TRUE GHOSTS

TRUE GHOSTS

Compiled by Christine Bernard

Armada

True Ghosts was first published as
The First Armada Book of True Ghost Stories
in 1974 by
Fontana Paperbacks,
14 St. James's Place, London SW1A 1PS.

This impression 1982.

*Many of these stories have been specially
rewritten for this collection.*

Printed in Great Britain by
Love & Malcomson Ltd., Brighton Road,
Redhill, Surrey.

CONTENTS

ACKNOWLEDGEMENTS

The editor gratefully acknowledges permission to reprint material used in this book to the following:

Messrs Cassell & Co. Ltd., and the executors of the late John Raynor, for an extract from A WESTMINSTER CHILDHOOD; also for material from THE STORY OF FULFILLED PROPHECY by Justine Glass

Robert Hale & Co. for material from Alasdair Alpin MacGregor's GHOST BOOK and Lauren Paine's A GAGGLE OF GHOSTS

William Collins Sons & Co. Ltd., for material from Lord Halifax's GHOST BOOK

Fred Gettings, Esq., for THE FRIENDLY MONKS OF GLASTONBURY ABBEY and GHOSTS IN PHOTO-GRAPHS. © Fred Gettings 1974

Acknowledgement is also due to the Österreichische Nationalbibliotek, Vienna, for permission to reproduce the photograph of Archduke Franz Ferdinand at Sarjevo.

About This Book

When starting to put together this collection I planned to tell you about haunted houses and their ghosts. But after reading hundreds of histories of gabled manors, battlemented castles and red-brick villas as well, I began to realize that ghosts are a pretty unoriginal lot. By this I mean that they all seem to go in for the same type of activities. How restless they are! What ever else they might or might not do, they certainly walk—and walk, and walk. And when they are not walking, they bang and thump about a great deal: knock on doors, drop heavy things, stomp about on attic floors. Of course, I liked some of the haunted house stories, and have included one about some noisy ghosts who haunted Billingham Manor on the Isle of Wight, also the story that tells of the unhappy young man who, for a hundred years, could find no peace in the Lion d'Or Hotel in Lille. But I decided that enough was enough, and began to explore other kinds of no less strange happenings.

Some ghosts have turned up over the centuries, not to haunt a house, but rather to attach themselves to a person or a family for a time, before disappearing again. Among them are the

American Bell Witch, tiresome Nelly Butler, and the extraordinary Talking Mongoose, all here to amaze and amuse you.

Did you know that there have been some pretty strong curses placed on both people and objects in our own century? I'd always thought that they went out with witches and broomsticks, but I was clearly wrong, as the case of the jinxed touring car shows. Strange things, too, have been revealed at seances, whether through a medium, or through automatic writing and table rapping. Fred Gettings, in his remarkable story about the monks of Glastonbury, tells of a successful contact made with the spirits of men who lived in the fifteenth century.

Many people deny the existence of ghosts altogether. They talk about 'leg-pulling', 'over imagination', and use various unpleasant words such as 'liar'! But since some experts believe that the gift of psychic sight is shared by only about ten out of every hundred people, it stands to reason that most of your friends and families will not be sympathetic on the subject of ghosts. Exactly what the gift of 'sight' is, few like to say. But I think that John Raynor, in his story about the poor musician, gives an entirely believable description of what it is like to be born with it.
NB Since a special vocabulary has grown up around the occult world, you may find it helpful to read the Glossary of Words on page 9.

Christine Bernard

GLOSSARY

FAKIR: The name for a wise and holy man in India; such a man can usually work magic.

GHOST: The spirit of a dead person appearing to the living.

MEDIUM: Someone who acts, willingly or unwillingly, as an intermediary between the spirit world and the ordinary material world we inhabit. Sometimes mediums work in a state of trance, at other times they work in a normal state of awareness.

POLTERGEIST: A playful or wicked spirit. Poltergeists always remain invisible, and their aim usually seems to be to tease or annoy people. They make sounds, move or throw objects, and sometimes (though rarely) hurt people. They can also introduce entirely new objects (such as lumps of coal, or stones) into a room.

PSYCHIC FORCES: The name given to a number of different kinds of energy, always invisible (unlike say, steam or water), which are connected with the appearance or sound of spirits and the spirit world. It is in fact a term loosely used to 'explain' mysterious happenings, for few people actually know what psychic forces really are.

SEANCE: A prepared attempt by an individual, or by a group of people, to make contact with spirits. It has been found that a strong wish among all the members of the group to contact spirits helps greatly. However, it is extremely unwise to conduct a seance without the presence of a well-trained medium, as certain evil spirits have been known to try and force their way into amateur seances and do much damage.

SPIRITUALISM: The belief that the spirits of the dead can communicate with, and sometimes show themselves to, the living.

TABLE-RAPPING: A kind of seance.

THE POOR MUSICIAN
(from *A Westminster Childhood*)

John Raynor

I was born on 5 June, 1909, at breakfast time. This caused my father displeasure, as he had to leave his boiled egg, which he had just cracked, upon hearing the news (but in any case he never cared to be disturbed at breakfast). The scene of my birth was in a room which was two tall flights of stairs above the dining room so that when my father at last got back to his egg it was quite cold, the toast flabby and the coffee bitter. Nor was a new meal possible as he had to begin teaching his class at nine. However, both he and I survived this unfortunate beginning.

My father was Master of the King's Scholars at Westminster School so I had the good fortune to live at Number 3, Little Dean's Yard, an eighteenth-century house in the inmost court of an inner court, the quietest and dreamiest place in London. Footsteps echoed sharply in the silence there, and the chimes of Big Ben and the clock of Westminster Abbey fell through the air like coloured stars against the hushed, distant traffic.

I inherited from my Scottish mother a deep awareness of unexplainable things; but then, she was the seventh child of a seventh child and any Scot will tell you that such a person is bound to have the 'gift of second sight'. As a small child I never questioned certain feelings and knowledge that I had, but accepted them as I accepted my ten toes or the colour of my eyes. If I 'knew' things that other people didn't, and was afraid of them, then that was how it was. The question 'do you believe in ghosts?' always interested me. I myself have never 'seen' one with my physical eyes—but with the inward eye I certainly have. And then again, I have certainly heard them with my physical ears and smelt one with my physical nose. Sometimes only a state of intense awareness is present, spinning horrible and black—or, occasionally, a crystal-clear and pure awareness. But I have often felt a 'presence'—a something that is going, very soon, to manifest itself . . .

Our house was huge, had four storeys and was old and rambling. There was a front staircase and a back staircase that was useful for escaping from punishment of some misdeed—but it was so horribly haunted that it was far worse than most ordinary punishments. Yet it was an exciting house to live in, full of unexpected cupboards and dark passageways, dimly lit at night. Every landing, every staircase, every room, had its own smell and atmosphere—and its own ghosts.

12

I cannot now remember exactly when I first heard the sounds, but I was certainly not more than four. I was sleeping in Nurse's room at the time of the first sound, right at the top of the house.

One night I was lying awake, sleepless, when a strange, quiet metallic buzzing started. I listened for a moment, and then my heart began to beat furiously, and I buried my head under the bedclothes. Still I could hear the sound, as clearly as before. I turned and twisted, trying to escape from it, but in vain. Then suddenly it stopped; and after a few moments, when I felt fairly certain that it would not start again, I fell asleep. From then onwards, night after night it would come, and I would lie awake, sometimes for hours, waiting for it, while the night-light burned steadily away in its saucer of water, and suddenly with a splutter and heave of flame would go out and plunge the room in darkness. Then the noise would start, the quiet but penetrating musical buzzing, sometimes high, sometimes low, but always constant in volume. It was filled with sadness rather than fear, and I think that I knew it was powerless to harm me, for I never felt for it unreasoning terror, only a kind of sick awe, and a devout hope that it would not start.

About a year later I was promoted to my brother Harold's bedroom, and it was there that

I heard an infinitely more terrible sound. Again, I was lying sleepless in bed when it started. It was like the other sound but was greatly intensified, and seemed to come from far away in the street, from the foot of the bed, and from inside my own head, at one and the same time. The sound itself was a terrible whirring flutter, minute yet loud, the embodiment of all hatred and fear. It would rise like a little angry scream and die away to a low moan. It was completely aware of me. The first time I heard it I was paralysed with fear; I lay under the bedclothes shivering in uncontrollable spasms. It was term-time, Harold was away at school and I was all alone. I tried to call for Nurse or Mother, but the steady waves of fear that gripped my throat prevented any sound coming out. At last it stopped, but for a long time I lay awake, staring into the darkness, till at last I could fight against tiredness no longer.

The noise—or rather, the *waiting* for the noise —began to play havoc with my nerves. For nights at a stretch it would be absent; sometimes for as long as a week; then suddenly, without warning, there it was. I would be warm and drowsy, on the point of falling asleep, and suddenly that vile fluttering whine would start, from the bed, from the street, from my head, infinitely far away and as near me as the pillow. After a time I managed to tell Mother about it, and she would come and sit by my bed until I fell asleep.

Then, after she had gone right downstairs again, I would sometimes suddenly wake and lie still for a moment, burdened with a dreadful knowledge; and tense, shrunk within myself, I would hear it start. It seemed to have some kind of intelligence, for on Friday nights, when mother had to attend a meeting, it never failed to put in an appearance.

For several months I was tormented. I grew pale and thin, and no one knew why. At that time I had no way of expressing the full extent of my feelings. The climax arrived suddenly in the early summer of 1914. Mother had suggested that the sound was probably due to one of the chimney-cowls in the yard turning in the wind on unoiled bearings. I tried my very hardest to believe this, and the knowledge that that was what Mother thought succeeded in slightly easing my fear.

Then, one night early in June, I woke suddenly to hear that sound very loud and clear. I got out of bed, shivering with fright, climbed on to the chest of drawers, drew back the curtains and looked out of the window, determined to prove to myself whether the sound did indeed come from a turning cowl. It was a night of brilliant moon; the yard and the Abbey shone spectrally cold and clear. Every cowl was visible in the flooding light. The night was absolutely still and silent, breath-held in its utter tranquillity. And no cowl was moving.

The most terrible horror I have ever known seized me; the sound rose in pitch, fluttering with shrill evil, on and on, clear, deathly and small. Crouching there on the chest of drawers, the last pretence of comfort removed, I began to scream and scream uncontrollably. The sound brought Nurse hurrying to me; she looked at me and ran to fetch Mother. Without a word I was lifted down, safe at last in comforting arms, and carried straight to Mother's bed for the rest of the night. In the morning a doctor came and talked to me and smiled kindly down upon me. In the afternoon I was taken into the country, to spend the next six weeks with my grown-up sister Edith.

Years later Mother mentioned to me that the doctor, puzzled beyond words, had in-insisted on this immediate change of surroundings, as I was in great danger at the age of five, of a nervous breakdown. And no one understood, except, probably, my mother, the real reason.

When I grew up, and only a few months before her death, my mother and I were talking together one day. We had somehow got on to the subject of ghosts, a subject that Mother intensely disliked. I asked her to tell me anything she knew about our house and the College.

She hesitated. "What do you want to know?" she asked.

"What you felt," I said.

"It was a terribly haunted house; you knew that?"

"Yes," I said.

"I tried to make them feel happier," she said unexpectedly. I waited. "The little boy in the drawing-room was terribly unhappy. I used to talk to him but nothing seemed to make it much better. Twice in the thirty years I lived there, I saw him. He was about eleven, and he wept bitterly and silently. Then there was your sister's room. I don't know—I never felt much there. But Father told me how he once slept there before I married him; and though he fought it, he had to get up in the middle of the night and make a bed for himself in another room."

"Why?" I asked; "what did he see?"

"I don't know," Mother replied; "he never would tell even me."

Mother was silent for a moment. Then she said, with extraordinary passion: "College Dormitory—oh, how I hated that. The smell, and the brooding, and the other-world feeling—oh, it was hateful. There is a story about that, you know," she said slowly. "A boy died in College. He was about fifteen. He was ill, and was put to bed and looked after in the room at the top of the house. This poor boy played the jew's harp. He's supposed to come through from College into our house and wander about between the back stairs and Nurse's room, playing his jew's harp. He's been seen and heard. I never met him myself, and I never heard him." She stopped and looked at me.

"You're white," she said. "I wish you hadn't made me tell you all this."

"I'm very glad," I said. "I can't think why you never told me earlier. Did you know about Harold's room, where I heard that terrible sound?"

"No," she said. "Nothing. But I didn't always care for the feeling of it; and it is supposed to be the oldest part of the house."

"Did this boy play the jew's harp well?"

"I believe he's supposed to be a very indifferent performer," said Mother. I smiled. Suddenly, looking closely at me, she said: "You heard him! Oh John, when?"

"When I slept in Nurse's room."

"Did you ever see him?"

"No. But why didn't you tell me all this? It would have explained so much."

"I didn't dare tell you," said my mother, "because I don't think, once you had known, you could have gone on living in that house. I was right, was I not?"

The following day I went out and bought a jew's harp, an instrument that I had never seen or heard, and took it to a friend who said he could play it. I suppose that he was right. He certainly played it better than the dead boy; but not a great deal better.

THE MAN IN THE IRON CAGE

This story was told to Lord Halifax, the Victorian ghost story collector. He heard it about seventy years after it happened to Miss Bessie Barrington in 1786.

My father and mother, with myself, my sisters and Charles my brother went abroad in the late autumn of 1786. We children were supposed to be learning French, and after visiting two or three towns our parents decided to make a longer stay at Lille. Besides finding the teaching good there, we had letters of introduction to some of the families in the neighbourhood.

The first lodging we had was very uncomfortable, so my father soon began to look about for a house. In due course he discovered one, very large and well-built, to which we took a great fancy. We were told that we could rent it for a remarkably low figure, even for that part of the world. So we took the house and moved into it at once.

About three weeks later I went with my mother to the bankers. As our money was paid out in large six franc pieces we could not take it with us and the banker offered to send his clerk. He asked our address and when we told him it was in the Place du Lion d'Or, he looked surprised. There was, he said seriously, nothing that would suit our family except indeed a house that had been long unlet because of a *revenant* (ghost) that walked about it.

My mother and I laughed, and as we were walking home my mother remarked in fun: "I suppose, Bessie, that it was the ghost which woke us up by walking about over our heads". I was sleeping in the same room with her and on three or four nights we had been awakened by a slow, heavy step overhead, which we thought must be one of the menservants walking about. The other women in the house were French, and so were the butler, the cook, the footman and a boy, Louis.

A few days after our visit to the bankers, having been again awakened in the night by steps overhead, my mother asked Cresswell, her maid, if someone was sleeping in the room over us. She replied: "No one, my lady. It is an empty garret."

A week or ten days later, Cresswell came in one morning after breakfast and told my mother that most of the French servants were talking of leaving because there was a *revenant* in the house. "Indeed, my lady," she said, "there is a very strange story about a young man who was heir to this and another house, with an estate in the country, who is said to have been confined by an uncle in an iron cage in this house. As he disappeared and was never afterwards seen, they supposed that he was killed here. The uncle left the house in a hurry and afterwards sold it. No one has ever remained in it for as long as we have, and it has been a long time without a tenant."

"And do you believe this, Cresswell?" asked my mother.

"Well," she replied, "the iron cage is in the garret over your head, my lady, and I wish you would come up and see it."

At this moment an old friend of ours arrived to call on us. We told him the story and asked him to accompany us upstairs. We found ourselves in a long, large garret, with bare brick walls. It was quite empty, except that in the farther corner there was an iron cage attached to the wall. It recalled to us the kind of cage in which wild beasts are kept, only it was higher, about four feet square and eight feet high. There was an iron ring in the wall at the back, to which was attached an old rusty chain with a collar.

We began to feel rather creepy at the idea that any human being could have been kept in such an unpleasant place, and our French friend was as horrified as we were. All the same, we were quite certain that the footsteps we had heard in the night were part of a plan to keep the house untenanted, and we were rather uncomfortable at the thought that there was a private way in, of which we knew nothing. We therefore decided to look about us for somewhere else to live.

About ten days after our visit to the garret, Cresswell came to dress my mother in the morning, looking so pale and ill that we asked her what was the matter.

"Indeed, my lady," she said, "we have been frightened to death. Neither Mrs. Marsh (my maid) nor I can sleep again in the rooms we are now in."

"Well," said my mother, "you may come and sleep in the little spare room next to ours. But what has frightened you?"

"Someone, my lady," she said, "went through our room last night. We both saw the figure, but hid under the bedclothes and lay in a dreadful fright till the morning."

I burst out laughing, but Cresswell began to cry, and when I saw that she was really upset I tried to comfort her. I told her we had heard of a very good house and would soon move into it. Meanwhile, they could sleep in the room next to ours. In the room in which they had been so frightened there was a second door which led to the backstairs, making it a kind of passage.

A few nights after the change of rooms my mother asked Charles and me to fetch her long embroidery frame from her bedroom. Although it was after supper and quite dark, we did not take a candle, as there was a lamp at the bottom of the staircase and we thought we could find the frame by leaving open the door of my mother's room. When we reached the foot of the stairs we saw a tall thin figure in a powdering gown and long hair going up the stairs in front of us. We both thought it was Hannah and called out, "It won't do, Hannah. You can't frighten us". At these words the figure turned into Cresswell's old room and when, in passing it, we saw nobody there, we concluded that she had gone through Cresswell's room and down the back staircase.

When we returned with the frame we told my mother of Hannah's trick. She said, "That's very odd. Hannah went to bed with a headache ages ago." We went at once to Hannah's room, where we found our maid, Alice, at work, and she told us that Hannah had been sound asleep for more than an hour. A little later, on our way to bed, we saw Cresswell. When we told her of our mistake she turned white and exclaimed: "That is exactly the figure we saw!"

About this time my brother Harry came to spend ten days with us. He was sleeping up another staircase at the far end of the house and one morning, when he came down to breakfast, he asked my mother quite angrily if she had thought he was drunk the night before and so

unable to put out his candle. Had she sent someone to spy on him? He added: "I jumped up
and opened my door and by the moon through
the skylight I saw a fellow in his loose gown at
the bottom of the stairs. If I had had anything
on I would have been after him and taught him
to come spying on me."

My mother was much upset, and could only
assure him that she had not sent anyone.

The next day a Mr. and Mrs. Atkyns and their
son, who lived three or four miles from Lille,
came on horseback to call on us. We told them
how frightened we had been, and how disagree-
able it was to be in a house which a person
might enter unknown to us. We told them that
no one would sleep in the room in which Cresswell and my maid had seen the *revenant*. Mrs.
Atkyns laughed, and said that with my mother's
permission she would like to sleep there and that
with her terrier to keep her company she would
not be in the least afraid. On my mother
replying that she had no objection, Mr. Atkyns
rode home with the boy to fetch his wife's
things.

In the morning Mrs. Atkyns looked ill and did
not appear to have slept much. When we asked
her if she had been frightened, she declared that
she had been roused from a sound sleep by
someone moving about her room. The dog did
not stir although he generally flew at an intruder,
but by the lamp in the chimney she distinctly

24

saw a figure. She said that she had tried to set the dog at it, but our belief was that she was much too frightened, and we were greatly entertained when Mr. Atkyns arrived to take her home and, to her indignation, said "Perhaps you dreamt it all."

After they had gone my mother said, as she had often done, "I cannot for an instant fancy it is a ghost, but I most sincerely hope I shall get out of the house without seeing what seems to frighten people so much; I know that to see any person in my room at night would alarm me dreadfully."

Three days before our move into the new house I had been for a long ride and went to bed tired. It was hot, and the curtains of our bed were undrawn on my side and at the foot. I was sleeping soundly when I was awakened, though by what I could not say (we were so accustomed to the footsteps overhead that by this time they never awakened either my mother or myself). We kept a light always burning in the room, and by it I saw a tall, thin figure in a long gown. One arm rested upon the chest of drawers that stood between the window and the door. The face was turned towards me; it was long and thin and pale, the face of a young man with a melancholy look which I shall never forget. I was very frightened, and I lay for nearly an hour before daring to look again towards the chest of drawers. When at last I did so I could see nothing, though I never heard the door opened or shut, or any other noise.

I did not close my eyes for the rest of the night, and when Cresswell came in as usual I called out, "I need not get up to let you in, for you must have forgotten to put the key upon the chest of drawers last night." She said she had not forgotten and, to my surprise, when I got up, I found the key in the usual place. When I told my mother, she was most grateful that I had not wakened her and insisted that we should not run the risk of spending another night in the house. So directly we had had breakfast we set about moving all our things, so that never again would we have to sleep in the Lion d'Or. Though before we left Cresswell and I examined every part of our room, we couldn't find any secret way of entering.

Some time later the following letter was sent to Lord Halifax by Baring-Gould, the author, who had received it after writing an article about the Man in the Iron Cage in the Cornhill Magazine.

Dear Mr. Baring-Gould,

The November number of the *Cornhill Magazine* has only lately come into my hands. I find your story of 'the Man in the Iron Cage' particularly interesting because of an experience I had at the Hôtel du Lion d'Or at Lille some thirty years ago.

In May 1887, I was travelling with two friends from Boulogne to Brussels. One of them, an aged lady unaccustomed to long railway journeys, became so tired that her sister decided it would be best to stop short at Lille and spend the night there. We arrived towards evening. Knowing nothing of the place and intending to go next morning we asked for the hotel nearest the station, which proved to be an old-fashioned inn, the Hôtel du Lion d'Or.

We were soon settled in a comfortable suite of rooms on the first floor. The larger bedroom communicated with my room. At first we thought this was the only entrance to my bedroom, but on examination we found a second door, at the farther end of my room. This, the landlord said, was usually kept locked. My friend, however, insisted on the door being unlocked and the key left in our possession. It opened into a small recess off the landing opposite the head of the stairs. This recess appeared to be used as a housemaid's closet, full of pails and brooms.

My friends retired very early to rest; since I did not feel at all tired, after wishing them good night I sat down in my room to write some letters home. The time slipped away quickly and it must have been between eleven and twelve o'clock when I became aware that, although the house had long been perfectly quiet, someone was walking up and down in a stealthy manner, just outside the door which opened into the recess. The 'slow, dragging steps' mentioned in your story exactly describes the sound I heard.

I paid little heed to it, thinking the steps were those of some belated servant. Suddenly there was a knock at the outer door of my room and the younger of my friends, whom I had thought asleep hours before, looked in, anxiously asking if anything was the matter, as she had been awakened by hearing me walking up and down. I assured her that I had not stirred from my chair and that I too had been surprised at hearing the same noise, which seemed to come from outside my door on the landing. We opened this door and with a light examined the recess and then the landing, but no one was to be seen.

We decided, rather nervously, that, although the footsteps seemed to have been so near, the sound must really have come from above, and we finally re-locked the door. My friend returned to her room and I went to bed, still hearing from time to time, until I fell asleep, that stealthy, dragging step.

We left Lille by an early train next day and I thought little more of this. It did not, however, completely pass from my mind, as I mentioned it on my return home about two months later. Then, a friend of my mother's, who knew of her interest in ghost stories, gave her a written description almost exactly similar to yours, of a haunted house in the Place du Lion d'Or at

Lille. It then struck me that this was the very house in which I had spent the night and that the footsteps I had heard were not those of any living person.

I have given you this account, thinking it may help you identify the house to which your sad story is attached.

Believe me to remain,

Yours faithfully,

A.C.

THE LATE NELLY BUTLER

Machiasport is an old New England town in America lying close to the village of Machias. The whole area, which lies to the north of the State of Maine, has many old houses in it, some dating back to the first settlers in New England. The people of Machiasport were God-fearing, industrious, stubborn and canny. In the early days of the American nation they were mainly of Scottish, Irish and English descent. Some of the things they most detested were Tory Englishmen, all Frenchmen, redskins—and occult matters. Not many years had passed since witches had been terribly persecuted in New England and in many cases burned at the stake. They had no wish to be reminded of this

In 1799 there lived near Machiasport one Abner Blaisdel, a man with a fine and untarnished reputation, an honest, reliable fellow and a staunch member of the church.

On the night of the 9th August, 1799, a disembodied voice suddenly announced loudly and abruptly in the Blaisdel home that an apparition was shortly going to appear. Abner, mindful of the results if his neighbours were told of this event, imposed a strict rule of silence on the members of his household who had heard the disembodied voice.

For five months nothing happened. The Blaisdels, although at a loss to explain it, began to wonder if in fact they had heard a voice at all. Then, on the 20th January, 1800, the voice spoke out again, strongly and purposefully. It belonged to a woman. She said she was the deceased wife of a neighbour, Captain George Butler. Her maiden name had been Nelly Hooper, daughter of David Hooper. The voice told the Blaisdels to send someone at once for 'its' father, old David Hooper, who resided some six miles away.

It was a nasty night, cold and bitter. The six-mile trip was not going to be pleasant, and yet there was no question that the disembodied voice belonged to someone, or something, that would stand for no excuses. The trip was duly made. Later, shaken but gratified after speaking with Nelly, David Hooper signed a statement that the visitor had given "such clear tokens of her being the spirit of my own daughter that I could only feel admiration and delight".

Until now, Nelly had been simply a voice; but later that same month, Abner's son Paul was crossing a field, and saw in the distance the silhouette of a woman. She came directly towards him, seeming, so he said, to float rather than walk. Paul, unable to speak, stood silent until she had passed. That was the first sighting of what became known as 'The Spectre', otherwise Nelly Hooper Butler. The following evening Nelly appeared in the house, scolded Paul for not speaking to her, and vanished. There were two obvious factors about those events. One: Nelly had evidently come to stay. Two: after David Hooper's excited recitation of his daughter's return, Abner's excellent reputation was in danger.

Nelly did not reappear during February, to the Blaisdel's relief, but in March she returned and in her imperious manner insisted that Abner, Paul and their wives go to talk to her—in the cellar! No one was at ease in the cold and dark cellar, but Nelly talked for two hours, in spite of the discomfort, and during this time told the Blaisdels that although her body had turned to dust in the grave, "my soul is as much alive as before I left the body".

As before, Nelly did not return for a month, but in May she was back again, and this time was seen by several people. She was also distinctly heard by others, and a great number swore that while they had heard a loud voice they could not distinguish the words. All this helped to save Abner's reputation, but he and his family said candidly they wished Nelly would do her visiting elsewhere. But at least it was no longer possible for people to laugh at the Blaisdels only. In fact as time passed and Nelly busily appeared in a number of different places, people were becoming seriously concerned with who, and what, Nelly was.

When Nelly first appeared, even before she became visible, the Blaisdels, adults and children alike, were very much afraid of her. The children moved their beds into their parents' room and acted as subdued as any frightened children would act. This annoyed Nelly and she spoke to the youngsters, saying, "Be not afraid, you need not be. I haven't hurt you, have I? And I shall not hurt you now, so put your things back in place." The children's beds were duly moved back where they belonged, and Nelly never did, in fact, harm the children—nor anyone else, although her presence more often than not caused goose pimples and fluttery hearts.

There were three remarkable things about this ghost. First, that she usually wore a long, loose-fitting white dress. Second, that when she was finally visible people who had known Nelly Hooper alive recognised her at once. Third, that shrill, bossy Nelly had not mellowed after death and showed the same curiosity about other people's affairs she had shown in life.

Nelly's notoriety spread and the Blaisdels had to play host to a stream of neighbours and total strangers; this, added to their other discomforts, did not make them any fonder of Nelly, whose liking for their cellar suggested that she found it ideally suited to her purposes. At one of those cellar meetings in early August of 1800, a visitor named Mary Gordon said, "I heard such a voice speaking to us as I never heard before or since. It was shrill but mild and pleasant." Later Nelly appeared. Mary Gordon recorded that event thus:

At first the apparition was a mere mass of light; then grew into personal form, about as tall as myself . . . she passed and repassed, so that any of us could have touched her. Yet when she passed by me she was so near that if there had been a substance I should have certainly felt it. The glow of the apparition constantly vibrated. At last the personal form became shapeless— expanded and then vanished in a moment.

Nelly, who hadn't done too much harm up to now, caused a scandal when she ordered her former husband George Butler to marry Lydia Blaisdel. Everyone in the Blaisdel household was shocked. These two, having been mildly attracted to one another before Nelly interfered, were suddenly embroiled in a family quarrel, for Abner refused to agree to this match. Lydia, too, refused to consent, or even to see Captain Butler again. Butler, on the other hand, was willing; when he pressed Lydia, not un- reasonably, she told him that under no cir- cumstances would she marry a man who had been frightened into proposing to her by a ghost!

Captain Butler insisted that his proposal was genuine; Lydia wavered, but when some sceptics said there was no ghost, and that Lydia Blaisdel had been dressing up as one to get George Butler to propose to her, she was furious. She decided to go away, to leave the area completely. Captain Butler had had about all he could stand; he followed Lydia, and in the end persuaded her to change her mind. Love won the day and they were soon married.

To the dismay of those who had claimed Lydia had been imitating a ghost to catch a husband, Nelly continued to appear. In fact she was more active than ever. But she also visited Captain Butler to inform him his bride would not live past their first year of married life. She was correct: ten months after marriage Lydia gave birth to a child and died the day after. Another time, when Abner Blaisdel asked about the health of his father who lived at a distance in York, Maine, Nelly without hesitation replied that the elder Blaisdel was dead. Abner wrote off at once and shortly afterwards received a reply confirming that his father had died seven days prior to the day he asked Nelly about him.

Among those who firmly rejected Nelly from the first, even though they saw her and recognised her, was Nelly's married sister, whose name was Sally Wentworth. Sally was of the opinion that the spectre who looked, acted and even spoke like her sister was a reasonable copy, hand-crafted in hell by the Devil!

Nelly now appeared to be quite devout, but

in life those who had known her had never considered her a religious person. Her own explanation was that she had felt the presence of God on her deathbed. In fact Nelly never failed to have an answer for anything; she was very forthright and opinionated, and although she could certainly tell of some events before they had occurred, she did not have any really startling revelations or prophecies to offer either. She seemed, in fact, to be very little changed from the way she had been in life.

Once, energetic Nelly organised a hike. She had all the people at the Blaisdel residence line up two by two and march out across the countryside for a mile or more, then march back again. In this procession was her successor, Lydia Blaisdel Butler, who walked with her discomforted husband. Nelly floated along beside George and Lydia all the way out and all the way back!

Nelly Butler was visible and audible for about one full year. As 'The Machias Ghost' she attracted considerable attention, caused a large number of statements—all essentially agreeing—to be written and signed by an entire community that had known her in either, or both, of her forms. Then she simply stopped either visually or audibly appearing alive or ghostly, and was never seen or heard of again!

If Nelly Butler was simply an ordinary, everyday ghost, what force, or lack of force, induced her to fade away? It seems highly unlikely that an entire community would see the identical hallucination, or that, if she were simply the result of imaginings, she would have been able to do or say the things she did.

Nelly was not a *welcome* apparition, yet this did not bother her one bit; even for those people to whom she wouldn't talk, there was one disturbing fact that could not be disputed: Nelly was just as blunt, nosy and domineering in death as she had been in life; she was, in fact such a perfect example of her living self that everyone who had known her on earth was forced to admit that Nelly hadn't changed one little bit.

THE HELPFUL MONKS OF GLASTONBURY

Fred Gettings

The counties of Wiltshire and Somerset are rich in tales of ghosts and other spirits. In this curious part of the world, you cannot go far without finding enormous standing stones, or dolmens, and the village of Avebury—near my home—is itself built in the middle of a stone circle. Many people believe that the stones were put there by magical means, long before the time of the Druids.

Not far along the main road is Marlborough, the birthplace of an archaeologist named Frederick Bligh Bond. In 1907, Bond was given the task of digging up the remains of Glastonbury Abbey, in Somerset, so that the original walls, which had been pulled down in the sixteenth century, could be reconstructed. How he was helped in his endeavours by spirits of those who had lived in the Abbey hundreds of years before makes a fascinating story.

As Bond was having great difficulty in finding the place where certain remains were buried, a friend suggested he might try to contact the spirits of the monks who had lived in the Abbey, to see if they would help. And so, in Bristol on a November night, Bond tried to contact these spirits by means of automatic writing. This is a means of communication with the spirit world through a pencil or pen held very lightly in someone's hand. Their hand is allowed to be moved by any force which wishes to do so. Sometimes, in this way, the hand will move entirely by itself, and the pen will write or draw pictures. (Almost always this is done by spirits.)

Immediately Bond began this automatic writing, a spirit started to write 'through' the pen. He said his name was Johannes Bryan, and that he was born in 1497. Johannes explained that he wanted to help Bond restore the Abbey, as he had been very fond of it when he had lived there. He had died just before Henry VIII had passed his laws ordering the destruction of the monastery, but it was clear from what he wrote that he knew just about everything that had gone on there since his death. He wrote in a curious English, and sometimes in Latin, but it is clear from his texts that he had never been a good Latin scholar. He admitted later that he preferred fishing, or just lazing about in the Abbey grounds, to being a serious and devout monk.

Johannes and his friends kept in close touch with Bond for several years, and particularly between 1907 and 1912 they helped him with advice on where and how to dig, in order to reconstruct their monastery. They told him many remarkable things: the name of the man who had finally pulled down the Abbey, and the exact measurements (afterwards found to be correct) of walls and arches, and they also helped him to find three secret passages, which to this day have not all been fully explored.

Bond always saved the scripts which had been written during the many seances with the spirits of the monks, and two stories—one about the sculptor who made fun of his Abbot, and the other about the dismembered skeleton—are perhaps the most extraordinary of all.

One day in 1908 Bond was walking to the village of Glastonbury, towards the Church called St. Benedict's (a church in fact dedicated to Benignus, a friend of St. Patrick, who first came to this area in the fifth century). As he walked, Bond glanced up at the west side of the tower, and he saw a curious carving in stone. It was the head of an Abbot, wearing a mitre. From this angle, it looked just like the profile of a mitred head. Bond assumed that it was the portrait of the Abbot Bere, who had rebuilt the church in the early sixteenth century. But he was puzzled, for he had not noticed the head before.

When Bond reached the church, he turned down the village street, and glanced upwards at the figure once more, and to his surprise he found that it had changed into a gargoyle! From this new angle directly below, instead of being the profile of an Abbot, it looked like a monstrous creature with a grotesque face and arched back, with prominent bones on its spine. Once he had got over his surprise, he decided to ask the spirit monks about this figure, to see if they knew anything about it.

As soon as Bond put the question to the monks he was astonished to have another monk make contact through the pencil. This one turned out to be the very monk who had carved the gargoyle. Like the others, he wrote in a curious sixteenth-century script, which is hard to read, and so the following is a modern version of what he wrote:

My name is Johannes Lory, and I am the Master Mason of the Guild of St. Andrew. Whilst carving the gargoyle of St. Benedict's in October, I found that my hands were too cold to work, so I came down from the ladder to walk about and warm myself. When I turned back to look at my carving, I saw that it looked like an Abbot. So I went back up to the carving, and worked on it until it looked like our own Abbot Bere. Everyone who saw it agreed that it was just like him. I did not really mean to make fun of him, and I didn't think that he knew about it.

The monk was obviously sorry for his joke, and he finished up his note to Bond plaintively, with the words, *I meant no despyte, God wot!* In fact, it is unlikely that the Abbot Bere would have minded the joke one little bit, for he obviously had a sense of humour. When he himself wrote a short note to Bond, he chose to sign his name with a rebus (a drawing standing for a name)—and he drew a keg of beer!

The gargoyle Abbot, a joke made by a monk in the sixteenth century, and apologized for over four hundred years later, still exists. It may be seen on the tower cornice of St. Benedict's. My daughter Tiffany and I wonder how many people who look up at it know its curious history—or, for that matter, see the joke!

The story of the skeleton is also true, but it is far from being a joke. Bond tells us in one of his books that whilst digging out the debris from beneath a part of the ancient Edgar Chapel of Glastonbury they found some bones lodged behind a wall.

As was Bond's practice by this time, he asked the spirit monks about these remains. Johannes Bryan explained that these were the remaining parts of the body of the last Abbot of Glastonbury. This Abbot, who had succeeded Bere, had decided to resist the order of Henry VIII to close down the Abbey. As a result he was arrested and tried for treason, and eventually hanged, drawn and quartered—this being the terrible punishment for treason in those days.

The quarters of the Abbot had been put on public display in Bath, Taunton, Wells and Bristol, as a warning to other traitors. But the monks, who loved their Abbot dearly, went secretly at night in order to recover the four parts of his body, to give them a decent burial. Unfortunately, they were able to find only two of the quarters, and these they buried, with due ceremony, but secretly, so as not to anger the King. Johannes said that they had buried the Abbot under the altar. Some time later, however, when the Abbey was being demolished, the workmen found some bones, and since they did not know to whom these belonged, they simply buried them behind the wall. It was here that Bond's workmen found them, in our own century.

When I first read this story, I had been very impressed by something the monks had said in their long account of the secret burial. One sentence in particular caught strangely at my memory, for the monks had written, *He swam in ayre when he would not.* I could only suppose that this meant that the Abbot had been hanged, or 'swam in the air on the end of a rope', because he refused to obey the King. However, the words were curious—one does not usually describe someone hanging as 'swimming in the air'. I was puzzled, and so I decided to look into this curious business. I therefore spent some time working in the British Museum, where so many ancient records are stored, and eventually I found what I wanted.

It seems that in the fifteenth century, long before the Abbot had been hanged, there had been a famous prophecy. It ran: *The time will come when a whiting will swim over the tor at Glastonbury.* As the whiting is a fish, and as the tor is a hill near the Abbey, and the highest point around, it was believed that the prophecy referred to a second flood. It was argued that if a whiting was able to swim high over the land, then the greater part of England would be covered in water, as in the days of the Biblical Flood.

Now the prophecy made perfect sense to me. The words written by the monks about their Abbot who had 'swum' in the air, were perfectly clear. The Abbot had been hanged on Glastonbury tor; he had 'swum' in air, and was likened to a fish because his name was Henry *Whiting*!

THE ENCOUNTER

The strange experience of the Reverend Spencer Nairne as told to Lord Halifax.

In the year 1859 I went on a cruise to Norway in a yacht belonging to my cousin. Our party consisted of an Edinburgh M.P. and his wife, his sister, his cousin, John Chalmers and myself. The other members of the party were all distant relations of mine, but they being Scottish and I English, I had not previously met them. We were to start from Edinburgh, the yacht coming up the west coast of Scotland and we had arranged to join her at Thurso. We all left Edinburgh by steamer at 8.0 a.m. on Tuesday, May 31st, arriving at Aberdeen at 4.0 p.m. the same day. I had never been there before. We went about the city, seeing its places of interest, and had high tea together at an hotel about 6.30 p.m. When we had finished we went out again to while away the time until 9.30 p.m., when we were to rejoin the steamer to continue our voyage to Thurso.

We walked up the main street of the town, which I think is called Union Street. It was about 8.30 in the evening and it was still full daylight (at Thurso there is blue sky at midnight). The street was quite crowded with people, walking on the footpaths in both directions. I was arm-in-arm with John Chalmers, and while we were walking and talking there passed me, going in the opposite direction, a lady whom I recognised as a Miss Wallis. She was not a close friend, but I had known her since my childhood (I was then twenty-six). She had been governess to some little cousins of my own age and had been so much valued and beloved that after they had grown up she had lived as governess-companion or visitor in one or other branch of that family. I very seldom saw her, but had a great regard for her and would never have seen her without going out of my way to speak to her—as of course I did now. She passed close enough to touch me. The path being crowded I did not see her until she was near me. She was walking with a gentleman, holding his arm and talking animatedly to him. I saw plainly that as she passed she certainly saw and recognised me.

I at once dropped my friend's arm and turned round to speak to her, fully expecting that she would do the same. Not only, however, had she not done so, but so far as I could see, she had completely disappeared. I looked everywhere, up and down the footpath and across the road, I walked quickly back in their direction and then turned back again, but not a sign of her could I see. I also looked into a good many of the shops in the immediate neighbourhood and was quite sure that she had not gone into any of them.

At ten o'clock we left Aberdeen in the steamer and I did not give much further thought to the encounter. We were in Norway until the 5th of September, sailing on that day from Stavanger. We landed at Aberdeen on Thursday, the 8th September, after dark, and left for Edinburgh by train early the next morning. I had therefore no opportunity of returning to the spot where I had seen Miss Wallis, but in any case the curious incident had almost passed from my mind.

Some three weeks later I paid a call on some of my cousins who lived in Mecklenburgh Square in London. There I saw Miss Wallis, and immediately went over to her. But before I could begin she said: "Now I have a quarrel to settle with you, Mr. Nairne! You cut me in Aberdeen a little while ago."

Astounded, I assured her that I had done no such thing, that I had indeed seen her and was positive that she had seen me, but that when I turned round to speak, which I did immediately, she was gone. She replied that exactly the same had happened to her. She had turned round at once and I had disappeared.

I said: "You were walking with a gentleman and talking to him and I thought that you recognised me just at the moment of passing."

"Yes," she replied, "it is exactly so. I was

walking with my brother and called out, 'Why, there's Mr. Nairne. I must speak to him.' "

Odd though it was, we could throw no more light on the subject, so we dropped it and she began to ask me about Norway, enquiring how long I had been there. I replied that my visit had lasted for a little over three months, from June 6th to September 8th.

"Well," she said, "but when were you in Aberdeen?"

"On May 31st."

She visibly paled.

"But I was not in Aberdeen then!" she cried. "I spent a week there with my brother at the end of July. I noted my meeting with you in my journal and if I had it here now I could show you the actual entry. I have never been in Aberdeen before or since."

She then said that her brother lived some distance out of the city, that they never went there in the evening and that her meeting with me took place earlier in the day.

Feeling a little odd myself I replied that I too kept a diary and that this would prove that the day I saw her was certainly not in July. In fact, I knew it was Tuesday, May 31st. (In writing this account I have my journal in front of me and it verifies the dates which I have given.) Two very puzzled, bewildered people later left that house in Mecklenburgh Square, never to meet again.

I am extremely sorry now that I did not at once write out the story as I have written it here and send it to her. Some years afterwards, on the advice of some friends, I did write it out, but just about that time Miss Wallis died, and she never saw it.

I can only vouch for the complete truth and accuracy of all that I have written. I saw Miss Wallis so distinctly and her recognition of me was so unmistakable that to my mind the matter cannot be explained away as a double case of mistaken identity.

THE TALKING MONGOOSE

Christine Bernard

In years gone by the people living on the Isle of Man, cut off as they were from the mainland by the Irish Sea, had a language of their own. It was called Manx. This language has fallen into disuse, but some of the words remain in its place names. Doarlish Cashen, a remote old farmhouse, is one such. Doarlish means 'gap' in Manx, and Cashen's Gap was the name given to this house, perched on the side of Dalby Mountain on the west coast of the Isle of Man. Our story begins over forty years ago, in 1931, when a family called Irving were living there.

Mr. Irving was an educated man, who had travelled widely, and his house was rather better furnished than you might have expected, with comfortable chairs and pretty cushions; while on the walls were many pictures of other countries, one of a tattooed Maori Chief, and some street scenes in Istanbul. He knew German and some Russian, Arabic, Yiddish, even Hindustani. So, for a start, he was no ordinary farmer. However, like any other farmer, he looked after a flock of sheep and some goats and poultry, on his forty-five acres of rough grass. His wife was a tall, striking-looking woman who believed she had psychic powers. Their daughter Voirrey, thirteen years old when this story begins, was much the youngest of the family, her brother and sister having grown up and left home some years earlier. She was a tall girl with greenish-brown eyes and long fair hair who had no friends of her own age; she was very quiet and reserved.

Now Cashen's Gap had one unique feature. When Mr. Irving bought his bleak farmhouse he found it very draughty, exposed as it was to violent winds and having no trees or shelter of any kind around it. So he built a thin inner wall throughout the house of wooden matchboard, leaving a space of about a foot between the old walls and the new. This certainly warmed the house—and may, perhaps have had something to do with the extraordinary events that occurred over the next four years.

One September evening the Irvings were sitting round the fire in the living room. They were tired, and feeling ready for bed—particularly Voirrey, who had had a long day. She was always up first, making tea and milking the goats, and today she had been tramping the moors with Mona, her brown sheep-dog, and picking late flowers, mushrooms and bilberries. She had also found a couple of rabbits in the snares set by her father the previous evening. For the Irvings

51

were poor and depended largely on rabbit and their own chicken for their main food.

Suddenly they heard a tapping sound coming from the attic: tap, tap, tap. The noise stopped and little growling noises began.

"We must have mice," said Mrs. Irving.

"Sounds more like a weasel to me," said Mr. Irving. Voirrey as usual said nothing. But she looked thoughtfully at the ceiling.

Next day Mr. Irving climbed up to the attic and almost immediately found a little wooden carving, which he had picked up on his travels in India. He was astonished to find it there and was about to complain to Voirrey when he had an idea. He dropped it on to the wooden floor of the attic—and found it made exactly the same sound they had all heard the evening before—a sharp, wooden tap. Mystified and intrigued, he decided to leave it where it was for the time being.

That same evening the tapping came again, but this time louder. Then it became a running noise.

"That's no mouse!" Mr. Irving exclaimed. Immediately came the sound of a series of animal noises: barking, growling, hissing, and spitting. Suddenly there was a violent *crack*, as of a whip, but so strong that it set the pictures on the walls swinging. The family were thoroughly unnerved and quite speechless with apprehension by now—and even more so when Mr. Irving repeated the animal noises—only to find that the creature, whatever it was, was copying him. "Vow-vow!" said Mr. Irving. "Vow-vow" said the creature—and then, in a tiny, whistling high-pitched voice, said (yes, *said*), "dog!" When he had recovered from the shock Mr. Irving called "Meow!" and back came the answer: "Meow . . . cat!"

Mr. Irving and his family were carried away in wonder. An animal taking lessons in human speech! Of course they set about searching for this creature—every nook and cranny, behind every cupboard, in cracks and corners, though they were hampered by the wooden partition and could only feel a short way into its depths through one or two odd openings.

Over the next few days the experiment was repeated, not once but many times. At that time, however often Mr. Irving and 'it' conversed, none of the family could see it. They only heard the high, shrill, disembodied little voice—and various thumpings, tappings, and so on, all over the house. By the beginning of November 'it' spoke quite fluently, using all their daily words and lots of others. 'It' never stopped asking questions and had a huge thirst for knowledge. "One more question, Jim," it used to plead to Mr. Irving, "then I'll let you go to sleep." Voirrey, too, taught it all the nursery rhymes and by December the creature was speaking fluently. He told them, then, that for years he had understood everything that people said but that he could not speak until he was taught by Mr. Irving, who, incidentally, had begun to call him Jack.

Mr. Irving discovered that some twenty years earlier a nearby farmer—by an odd coincidence his name had been Irvine—had got hold of a number of *mongooses** and released them in the fields to get rid of a plague of rabbits. Yet, when Mr. Irving suggested that Jack must be the descendant of one of them, he said no, that he was "born on the 7th June, 1852, came from Delhi in India, and had been chased and shot at by natives"! In the first alarming weeks a state of war existed between the farmer and Jack and Mr. Irving confessed to feeling afraid. Was this a ghost? he wondered. Jack encouraged this belief and said, "I'm a ghost in the form of a weasel, and I shall haunt you with weird noises and clanking chains." (Which was really a very ordinary idea of a ghost!) Yet, around the same time, he also said, "if you are kind to me, I will bring you good luck. If you are not kind I shall kill your poultry. But I am not evil, though I could be if I wanted. You don't know what harm I could do if I were roused. I could kill you all if I wanted."

* Small, four-footed weasel-like creatures, common in India, able to kill poisonous snakes (see photograph in Plate 1).

At this stage the creature became aggressive and rude and developed a habit of throwing all kinds of things into the living-room with great force. This both frightened and angered the Irvings. Although no-one, still, had seen him, Mr. Irving decided that the time had come to get rid of Jack. But though one or other of them caught, out of the corner of their eye, a dim shadow of a bushy tail as it whisked out of sight, or perhaps a little paw thrust through a gap in the wall, no-one could actually claim to have seen Jack—so of course it was impossible to catch or kill him.

In this aggressive period his language, too, was terrible and Voirrey's bed was moved into another room, her parents hoping that she wouldn't be able to hear Jack's disgraceful vocabulary. But as this phase passed and the creature became less hostile, he began to go into fits of screaming, keeping the horrified Irvings awake and distraught for hours. The nights were full of groans and sighs, as of someone in agony. Then, as suddenly as he began, Jack stopped his nocturnal noises.

"What was all that ghastly screaming about, then?" Mr. Irving asked Jack, who had been quite silent for several days and had only now made his presence felt by a tiny scratching noise. The voice answered immediately: "I did it for devilment!"

Soon his behaviour greatly improved until he

became quite affectionate, speaking cheerfully to all the family. Now he changed his name to a softer version of Jack, asking to be called Gef—and the name stuck. When the Irvings occasionally mentioned leaving the house because the farm was not going too well, Gef grew alarmed. "Would you go away and leave me?" he asked.

"Yes," said Mrs. Irving. "You haven't helped us, though you promised to."

"I got rabbits for you," he said sulkily. This was true; quite often Voirrey found a dead rabbit near the back door, killed long before either she or Mona were up and about (during his years at Cashen's Gap Gef killed seventy-one rabbits for the Irvings).

Mrs. Irving replied "Maybe, but you promised to help us make money, and you haven't done so."

"No," said Gef, with both spirit and insight, "for if you make money you'll go away and leave me." He continued, "The house holds three attractions for me: I follow Voirrey, Mam gives me food, and Jim answers my questions."

Well, as you can imagine, it was not long before word of the astonishing happenings in the remote farmhouse reached the outside world. News of the mystery farmhouse reached London in October, 1931 when the *Daily Sketch* published a photograph of the Irving's cottage with the caption 'The Talking-Weasel Farm' while the *Daily Mail* and other newspapers reported strange events at Doarlish Cashen. Early in 1932 Manchester's *Daily Dispatch* sent a reporter to the Isle of Man, and this is what he wrote the next day in his column:

The mysterious 'man-weasel' has spoken to me today. Investigation of the most remarkable animal story that has ever been given publicity leaves me in a state of perplexity. Had I heard a weasel speak? I do not know, but I do know that I have heard today a voice which I should never have imagined could issue from a human throat; that the people who live there seem sane, honest, and responsible folk and not likely to indulge in a difficult, long-drawn-out and unprofitable practical joke . . . and that others have had the same experience as myself.

Soon after this Harry Price received a letter from Mr. Irving telling him of their strange new inhabitant. Harry Price and R. S. Lambert were two investigating officers for the Society of Psychical Research. At that time Mr. Lambert was editor of the B.B.C.'s *The Listener*. The Chairman of the London County Council said Mr. Lambert was crazy for believing in the 'Talking Mongoose'. Mr. Lambert, who had been as startled as you or I would have been if we had ever heard Gef, was naturally annoyed at being dubbed mad and promptly sued the Chairman. After a sensational trial he was awarded £7,500 damages: forty years ago this was a lot of money.

Over the next four years Cashen's Gap had a lot of visitors. Apart from many sightseers, Harry Price and R. S. Lambert came down to investigate and although they didn't see Gef they certainly heard him. Later they wrote a book about their investigations and called it *The Haunting of Cashen's Gap.*

Well, so who *did* see him? Mr. Irving wrote to Harry Price in 1932:

The animal has been seen by myself and daughter in one of the two bedrooms of my house on several occasions. My daughter has twice seen . . . its tail only, in the small back kitchen, in a hole in the wall. My wife has seen it only on one occasion. The colour is yellow . . . the tail is long and bushy, tinged with brown . . . my daughter says the face is all yellow, and the shape is more that of a hedgehog, but flattened at the snout like the domestic pig . . .

Gef described himself as 'a little clever, extra clever mongoose,' and was clearly very shy and nervous of being seen. His fingers were once seen through a crack near the ceiling and were 'short, yellow and the nails curved'. But Gef allowed all his fingers to be touched. Mrs. Irving was even allowed to stroke his fur and put her middle finger into Gef's mouth. "It seemed to fill it," she said. "His teeth were tiny and sharp. He drew a little blood from my finger. I was indignant. I told him : 'I don't want any blood poisoning.' He answered: 'Go and put ointment on it!' "

But many people, family, visitors, researchers, heard him. And he was certainly worth hearing. Indeed, this is one of the reasons I'm telling you the story of Gef. He said such extraordinary, funny things. Two local boys, Harry Hall and Will Cubbon, called on the farm one day. Harry told his story:

Mr. Irving told us that Gef can tell the head or tail of a penny if it is placed on the porch window. I took a penny from my pocket, tossed it and placed it on the window-ledge. As soon as I came back into the kitchen, Gef shouted "Tail". He was right. I tossed again. He was right again. Then, I did not toss again, but left the penny as it was. Gef said, "You did not turn the penny." The voice was a very high, screechy sort. I never heard one like it.

Sometimes Gef went away for days. He would roam the countryside, enter people's houses and listen to all sorts of private gossip. Folk were uneasy. "That mongoose knows far too much," they said. Once, mischievously, he threw gravel at the window of a lonely cottage. "The female was hiding behind a door," he reported back. "Then the father came out with a whacking big stick." Will Cubbon, one of the boys who witnessed the penny incident, reported that Gef asked him, "Can you drive a steamroller?" Will said yes, he could. Gef did not believe him. "You young rascal," he cried. "You would put it over a hedge. Clear to hell!"

Gef was very fond of the word 'hell'. After visiting a country estate twenty miles away he told the Irvings about his adventures when he got home. He had had, he said, "A hell of a job to climb over the wire net" which surrounded the estate. He had got there under a lorry and when the Irvings pointed out that he might have been seen, or killed by dogs, he replied: "Oh God, was I tired!" Asked how he dared to do it, he replied simply, "I watch like hell!"

Gef gathered much local information from listening to people talking in buses, under which, too, he always travelled. Hearing that the 'talking mongoose' was stealing bus rides the electrician at the town bus terminus cruelly set up a contact plate under the bus to electrocute Gef. Irving heard of this and warned Gef. "Oh," he replied carelessly, "I know all about it, it's under bus 81." Irving enquired and found that Gef's knowledge was entirely accurate.

His character—at least measured by the things he said—was by turns cheeky, quarrelsome, jeering, pathetic and brave. Here are some of the things he said that were recorded at various times, either by the Irvings or their friends. He would sometimes make the most absurd claims, rather like a small child's bragging: "I am the fifth dimension", and "I am the eighth wonder of the world". In his conversations with the Irvings he would speak as to a contemporary. "Hey, Jim," he would call to Mr. Irving when hungry, "how about some grubbo?" Having helped himself one day in the larder he called to Mrs. Irving: "Maggie, I hope you don't mind, I've eaten the bacon." One day he saw a box of chocolates that had been sent to Voirrey. He was asked if he was hungry and replied, "Yes, I will have some of those chocolates. A nut and a black paradise and a muck sweet!" Evidently he learned his words from listening to people and whenever he heard new words he would call, "Hey, Jim. What is 'countenance'? What is 'loco'? What is a 'nun'?" and would then shout back "Honest, Jim? Word of honour, Jim?" One day he saw Mr. Irving reading the Bible. "Look!" he cried to Maggie "Look at the pious old atheist, reading the *Bible*; he will swear in a minute." Most amusing of all, Gef was afraid of ghosts. Mr. Irving told an enquirer of an incident one evening:

While sitting on the bed, I heard Gef talking to my wife and daughter below. I put a sheet round my head, took off my boots and slipped silently downstairs. When I crept into the kitchen Gef screamed with fright; "Clear to hell!" When I took the sheet off he sobbed like a child.

Well, these and many other similar stories make up the extraordinary tale of the talking mongoose. Like so many other strange stories, this one too has an unsatisfactory ending. In the

61

last months of 1935, four years after Gef's sudden arrival, the Irvings sold Doarlish Cashen—and vanished. Gef might have gone with them—or of course, he might have died. In 1947 the new owner of the farm claimed he shot a queer-looking animal that looked like a mongoose; he thought it must have been Gef because, he said, the house was no longer haunted.

And what are we to make of Gef? A lot of theories were put forward at the time: that he was a ghost; a poltergeist; a 'familiar' from the world of witchcraft (and he does remind me a bit of Nellie Butler); or an earth-bound spirit in animal form. It is said that some Indian fakirs possess the power to make mongooses talk. And we mustn't forget those that had been released in the district twenty years earlier to kill the over-populous rabbits. Talking animals, from Balaam's ass to the Elberfeld horses, have long been with us and continue to puzzle mankind.

Whatever the explanation, a lot of people who were sane, intelligent rational human beings heard, not once, but several times a small lively creature talking like a human being—and talking very obviously with human intelligence behind his speech. No-one has been able to come up with a rational explanation, though you may think that a Dr. Maxwell Telling of Leeds did, perhaps, come nearer the truth when he said that Gef was "a missing link between the animal and human intellect". In earlier days there is little doubt that all three Irvings would have been burnt as witches. Because our ancestors *did* believe in an irrational and dangerous spirit world, and they never questioned their right to destroy those they considered agents of that world. But we, in our day, have cast away, perhaps to our loss, belief in both good and bad spirits, and can only believe what is rational, and open to scientific explanation. Perhaps it could be that every once in a while the powers of lightness and darkness send us reminders of the existence of another world of the spirit . . .

THE UNBIDDEN GUESTS

Alasdair MacGregor

One of the most pleasing houses within easy reach of London is the Old Court House, at Hampton Court, the home of Sir Christopher Wren during the last five years of his life. The house was remodelled by Wren, and at a later date probably by William Kent. In 1908 it became the home of my friend, Norman Lamplugh, and remained so for the next thirty years.

The house was frequently the scene of gay garden-parties, and the following ghostly incident occurred on a Friday afternoon in June, 1929, when such a party was in progress, and the house very full. Norman's brother, Ernest, and an artist friend, the Comte de l'Hopital, while standing on the landing, suddenly noticed among the guests a boy of about eight years of age— a pretty child with long fair hair. He threaded his way through the crowd. For two reasons this young visitor drew more than casual attention. In the first place, no children had been invited to the party; and in the second, he wore unusual clothes—the black-and-white costume of a page

Plate 1. *The Talking Mongoose* (p. 50) Above: a drawing of Gef. The artist was helped by descriptions given by the talking mongoose himself. It is interesting to compare the drawing with the photograph below of an actual mongoose in the London Zoo.

Plate 2. *Ghosts in Photographs* (p. 76) The picture of Tiffany taken when she was feeling sad. Perhaps it was because of this that the shadow spirit hand appeared to comfort her.

Plate 3. *Ghosts in Photographs* (p. 78) The Buxton family at Exmouth in 1923. The face of a smiling boy and the profile of a pony can be seen over the woman's head. The boy had died a year before the picture was taken, and the pony, Tommy (shown also in real life), some years earlier.

Plate 4. *The Jinxed Touring Car* (p. 119) Archduke Ferdinand and his wife Sophie at Sarajevo (back seat). In the middle, *l*, Governor Potiorek (the next owner of the car — he too became a victim of its terrible curse), and, *r*, Count Harrach. Minutes after this photograph was taken, a young revolutionary shot and killed the Archduke and his wife.

in the time of Charles II. From his shoulders hung a short, black-and-white cape. His breeches were of black velvet. His black shoes had large silver buckles and his stockings were of white silk. So you see, those who saw him did so very distinctly.

So close to Ernest Lamplugh and de l'Hopital did the child pass that they were obliged to step back a little in order to make room for him. He took no notice of them, but just walked on. The Lamplugh's sister, Ethel, now saw him outside the drawing-room door. She was equally surprised at seeing a child at their garden-party, and particularly one so quaintly dressed. The child took no notice of her either, nor indeed of any of the guests but passed quickly upstairs. As he went, Ethel Lamplugh pointed him out to her great-niece, Carol Done, who was standing quite close to her. Carol, however, could not see him.

That evening, after the party, as the Lamplughs and the Count sat talking, the matter of the strange and unidentified guest arose. All three who had seen him were agreed that there was something a little odd about the incident—something prompting investigation. They sent for the servants and questioned them, but not one of them had seen a child of any description enter or leave the house. Later, they made enquiries among their guests to ascertain whether any of them had brought to the party a child. No one had done so: nor had anyone *seen* a

65

child—and certainly not a child clothed in fancy dress!

Now, the little boy had been seen to walk upstairs to the top floor. In order to leave, assuming him to have been an ordinary human being, it would have been necessary for him to have descended the same way. This he had not done. Those who had seen him in his strange attire would certainly have noticed him, had he returned by the staircase. A search was made upstairs. No little boy could be found. Ethel and Ernest Lamplugh and the Comte de l'Hopital had undoubtedly seen the phantom of a child. All three described him and these descriptions were identical.

And now to the sequel. Of the three who had seen the little ghost, two Lamplughs, usually in excellent health, were soon taken ill: Ethel was seriously ill for a couple of years thereafter, and Ernest developed heart trouble which put him out of action for some time. Six months later, the Count (incidentally, he was the first to see the phantom visitor) died. He had always been passionately fond of children, and was continually painting them. Was the ghostly boy's appearance at the Old Court House the presage of illness and death?

All his life, Alasdair MacGregor has collected tales of ghosts and hauntings. The following story came to him through J. W. Herries, who was chief reporter of The Scotsman *for many years. He devoted a good deal of attention to psychic research, and wrote several articles and a book* on the subject. Herries regards this story, which occurred in 1936, as one of the most striking and unusual he has ever come across. He heard it from a Mr. Allan Thomas, who knew both of the principal characters, and who assured Herries that it was true in every detail.*

During some festivities at a country house in Devon, a young friend of Thomas's was a guest. When alone one evening in a room where the table was laden with excellent food, she saw a young man enter by a door to her left. He walked across the room. In doing so, he looked hard at her—while she looked at him. He left the room by a door to her right. His appearance so interested her that she asked her hostess about him. Despite her description, and her insistence that she had seen such a person, her hostess was quite unable to identify him. Yet, the girl was positive that she had seen someone enter and leave the room in the manner related. Who the 'guest' could have been, no one had the slightest idea.

At a party in London, two years later, the girl saw this elusive young man again. "But I met

* *I Came, I Saw*, published by Oliver & Boyd, Edinburgh, 1937.

you before, at such-and-such a house in Devon!"
she exclaimed, as they were being introduced.
The young man was very surprised, declaring
that he had never heard of the house, and that
he had certainly never been there. The girl,
however, remained convinced that she had seen
him before. "I certainly saw you there!" she insisted.

All this, as it turned out, provided grounds
for friendship. The two of them saw a great deal
of one another—and eventually they were married.

Shortly after the wedding, the young wife was
invited to bring her husband with her to the
Devonshire house on a short visit. The evening
they arrived there, she took him down to the
room where she insisted she had first seen him.
"This is where I saw you," she said. "I was standing here. You came in at that door, and went
out by the other."

The husband, looking round the room in some
amazement, assured her that he had never been
there before. This was the first time he had ever
been in the house, the first time he had ever entered that particular room. In so saying, he
passed across the room to make his exit by the
second door—*never to be seen again.*

Herries relates that he disappeared absolutely
from all knowledge. The B.B.C. put out a description of him, and sought information as to

his whereabouts, but without avail. From that day to this, nothing has been heard of him.

Alasdair MacGregor ends his story by saying: "What happened to the bereaved young wife? It would indeed be interesting if, by publishing this story, we were to hear from her!"

THE PASSENGER WITH THE BAG

One morning in the nineteen-twenties, a city gentleman by the name of Spears was leaving London by train from Euston. Having with him some papers which he wished to read during the journey, he asked if he might have a carriage to himself. The train was not full, so the guard found him an empty compartment and locked the door. Just as the train was about to start, an elderly gentleman, carrying a bag, appeared in a great hurry. He turned the handle of the door, which apparently had not, as the occupant of the carriage thought, been locked, and got in. After a little while, the two men fell into conversation, the last-comer informing his companion that he was a director of the railway company and was particularly interested in a branch line which was about to be opened. He added that he was carrying with him seventy thousand pounds in railway funds which he would place in a local bank.

"Are you not afraid," said Mr. Spears, "to carry about such a large sum?"

"Oh, no!" was the reply. "No one would know. Besides, who would rob me? Not you, just because I have told you. I am not afraid of anything happening."

They went on talking, and in the course of their conversation the gentleman with the bag said: "By the way, I know the house where you are going to stay. The lady is my niece. Will you give her my kind regards and tell her that I hope the next time I come to stay she won't have such a huge fire in the Blue Room as she had the last time? She nearly roasted me out! But here is my station."

The elderly gentleman rose and prepared to get out. Before doing so, however, he gave Mr. Spears his card, on which was the odd name of Dwerringhouse. He then left the carriage, and Spears, settling himself back in his seat, saw him walking down the platform with his bag. At that moment, he noticed a cigar-case lying on the floor close to his feet. Picking it up, he saw that Mr. Dwerringhouse's name was on it. Since the train was not due to start for another two minutes, he jumped out and ran along the platform in the hope of catching his recent companion. He had a glimpse of him standing under a lamp-post talking to a man at the end of the platform. He noticed that the man's hair was of a sandy colour and could plainly see his face, which was turned towards him. As he drew near, however, he lost sight of both the men, who seemed to have suddenly disappeared. Although he looked round carefully, there was no sign of them at all, and when he asked a porter what had happened to them the man replied that he had not seen any such people and that they could not have passed his way. The train was now about to start and the gentleman, very much puzzled, had to hurry back to his carriage.

Arriving at his destination that evening, he dressed for dinner and found a large party in the drawing-room. During dinner he remembered the message to his hostess, and turning to her said: "I travelled down with an uncle of yours and he told me to give you a message." Then he told her about his meeting on the train and the message he had been given.

The lady appeared to be greatly distressed and put out, and so was her husband; Mr. Spears realised that he had said something very unfortunate. But what it was or how he could have annoyed his host and hostess he could not imagine. However, when the ladies had retired from the dining-room, the husband took him aside and said: "Very awkward, what you told my wife, when you gave her that message from her uncle. The fact is he has disappeared and no one knows where he is. What is worse, he absconded with seventy thousand pounds. The police are looking for him and, as you can imagine, it is not a pleasant subject in this house."

Among the guests at dinner were two directors of the railway company. They approached Mr.

Spears later in the evening and asked him if he could give them any further particulars about this man whom he had met in the train.

"No," he replied, "I can tell you no more, except that I saw him and talked with him and left him, as I thought, speaking to another man on the station platform."

But the directors continued to press him and eventually asked him if he would mind appearing before their Board and telling his story to them. He agreed to do so and in due course the meeting was arranged. He was in the middle of his narrative when he suddenly exclaimed: "There is the man I saw talking to Mr. Dwerringhouse!—that man with the sandy hair!"

A man of this description was actually sitting among the directors. He was the cashier of the company, and now, taken by surprise, he called out: "But I was not there. I was away on my holiday."

Nevertheless, there and then the directors insisted upon the records being brought in and examined; from them it was clear that the cashier had not been away on his holiday at the time, in spite of what he said. They closely cross-examined him and eventually forced from him a confession. He admitted that he had murdered Mr. Dwerringhouse. He insisted that he had not meant to do so, but had known of the journey and of the money Dwerringhouse was carrying.

Having met him at the station, he had persuaded him to take a short cut and, when they were passing through a quarry, had knocked him on the head. He had only meant to stun him and so get possession of his bag, but in falling Mr. Dwerringhouse had struck his head on a stone and been killed.

The curious episode of the cigar-case was explained by the fact that, owing to some necessary repairs, the carriage in which Mr. Spears and Mr. Dwerringhouse had travelled had been out of use since he journeyed on the day of his murder. He must have dropped it then. Not until the day of Mr. Spears' own journey was the carriage, still containing Mr. Dwerringhouse's unnoticed cigar case, put back in use. The guard at Euston was positive that on the day of the 'appearance' he had certainly locked the door of the carriage but that *only one gentleman was inside when the train started*.

GHOSTS IN PHOTOGRAPHS

Fred Gettings

Some years ago, when my daughter Tiffany was about three years old, I took her one Sunday afternoon to visit a friend who lived in London. His house was in rather a grim and dreary terrace at Earls Court. It was raining when we arrived, and I remember that Tiffany was in a grumpy sort of mood. So, to amuse her, I stopped the car and we watched a man making a paper hat from a newspaper and then putting it on his head to keep off the rain. But the rain just collected in the hat and ran in a rivulet down his face. We got a bit wet too, as we scrambled from the car to the door of the house. I mention these facts simply to make it clear that this was just a normal kind of visit on a normalish sort of day —except that Tiffany was not her normal cheery self.

My friend is a university teacher and he liked to spend his Sunday afternoons talking to friends and giving them cream cakes and tea. Like most interesting people, he had strange ideas: for example, he believed that you could persuade flowers to grow by talking to them.

But in almost every other way he was a serious scientist, even quite an important one. I'm sure that he didn't believe in ghosts or what he would have called 'that kind of nonsense'. Certainly there was nothing spooky about his house. (If I had been a spirit I don't think I'd have chosen to haunt it—my friend's 'inventions' would have frightened me off. Especially the one for training flies to walk around the rims of coffee cups!)

Whilst we were having tea and, as I recall, talking about monkeys, another friend arrived. He had recently taken up photography as a hobby, and so we were not surprised when he insisted on taking photographs of everyone. We all posed for him, and afterwards we continued talking and eating. I remember he took one or two pictures of Tiffany, as she sat in a corner eating chocolate cake. After we left the house we forgot all about the photographer.

However, a few days later he telephoned me, said that something strange had happened, and asked me to meet him for lunch. As soon as I arrived he excitedly showed me a photograph of Tiffany, sitting in a corner of the room, with a spoon in her left hand, a cup of orange juice in front of her—and a spirit hand resting on her head! This photograph appears in Plate 2. A medium who deals with this sort of thing every day, told me that it was the hand of a guardian spirit comforting Tiffany because she was feeling unhappy that Sunday afternoon.

Most people think of spirits as being quite invisible, yet the fact is that thousands of photographs of them—sometimes very misty, sometimes looking as real as you or me—have been taken during the past hundred years. The earliest known picture of this kind was taken in 1861 by William Mumler, an American. He found, much to his surprise, that very often when he took a picture of a person, there would appear on the print an image of someone who was no longer living, as well as that of the sitter. Usually the spirit was closely related to the sitter. Mumler was not really interested in making spirit pictures. He was completely absorbed in the then new art of photography and was very upset when his employer almost sacked him for 'spoiling' the prints. It took Mumler a long time to persuade him it was quite unintentional!

When people heard of Mumler's strange gift they started flocking to the studio to have their photographs taken, hoping that pictures of departed family and friends would also appear. Perhaps the most curious story, among the many he tells in his autobiography is the one about a lady who visited him soon after the assassination of the great President Lincoln. The lady was very sad, and it was clear to Mumler that she was hoping for a picture of someone recently dead. When he developed the photograph he found, to his utter astonishment, that behind the lady, resting his hand on her shoulder, stood the transparent figure of Abraham Lincoln himself. The lady was the President's widow and, without knowing it, he had photographed the President of the United States in spirit form! Although Mumler continued taking such pictures all his life he was never able to explain how it happened.

Of course, not all spirit photographs are genuine, for there are always people keen to make money, or make some kind of reputation as spiritualists by faking pictures. One authority on the subject says that over two hundred ways of faking them have been discovered. Yet enough evidence has been produced to make it clear that a great number of pictures are genuine, even though no one can explain them. Today it is even possible to take pictures of ghosts in colour!

My favourite photograph of the spirit world, reproduced in Plate 3, is a rather remarkable one, for it includes spirits of both an animal and a human being in one picture. It was taken around 1923 near the seashore at Exmouth, and were it not for the cloudy shapes above the head of the lady it would be just an ordinary picture of a family sitting on the steps of a caravan on a day's outing. However, in the blurred images above her white-brimmed hat it is possible to see the head of a young boy, and next to him the head of a horse or pony. The heads of the boy and the pony are images from the spiritual world, and the family in the photograph knew them well.

After she had seen the curious results on the photograph, Mrs. Buxton, the lady in the picture, said that she had been thinking about her son. He had died in the previous year, and she was thinking that it would have nice if he had been there in the group, having the photograph taken along with his family. As it was, it seems he was there in a sense, for it is her son's face which appears in the cloud above her head.

The lady also recognized the pony. This was Tommy who had been one of the favourite ponies owned by her son during his lifetime. The pony had died some years earlier, but as you can see from the photograph of Tommy, taken when he was very much alive, there is a very close resemblance. The Buxton family who appear in the photograph are now convinced that their boy and Tommy are still close together in some way, and are happy about it.

But the most interesting of all ghost pictures are those taken by a scientist towards the end of the last century. He was called Sir William Crookes and was the inventor of several important pieces of apparatus, the editor of a famous scientific journal, the discoverer of thallium, and a man highly respected in the world of learning. He first came into contact with spirits in 1869, when he decided to make a scientific study of the many different kinds of seance which, until then, no scientists had bothered to investigate—though they were usually the first to laugh at them.

Sir William invited mediums to contact spirits, and while they were doing so he investigated their methods as closely as possible, with complicated equipment, in an attempt to find the truth. One medium caused a table to float around a room, another made a pendulum, locked in a glass case that had been cemented to the wall, to swing before the viewers' astonished eyes. Yet Sir William found he was quite unable to explain, scientifically, what was happening.

The most important—and baffling—piece of work which he conducted was with a medium called Florence Cook. This young lady was about fifteen in 1872, which was when she first became aware of the 'presence' of another girl. At first the presence was not clearly visible, but after a few months she had materialized completely and was able to talk to Florence for long periods of time. She said her name had been Annie Owen Morgan, and that she was the daughter of a famous pirate who had lived in the days of Charles I. She had been pretty wicked during her life—in fact she finally admitted that she had murdered her two children. But now she was trying to make up for her past crimes, she said, by helping the world to understand the truths of spiritualism. She wanted to change her name, and asked Florence to call her Katie King.

Altogether Katie spent three years with Florence, and appeared so frequently that she became almost one of the family. When Florence married, her husband said that he had not realized he had married *two* women; not surprisingly, he sometimes got quite angry that Katie should be around so often!

It was natural that Sir William Crookes should become interested in these strange appearances and he spent some time studying her and Florence. Sometimes he studied them together, noting, for example, the time it took for Katie to appear and disappear, while at others he tested both Florence and the room in which Katie appeared. And, most important, he arranged to have over forty photographs taken of Katie King; some of her alone, looking intense and beautiful, some with Florence, and yet more with himself and Katie. There they stand, a most unlikely pair: Sir William Crookes, one of the most important scientists of the day, serious of face, with a great bushy white beard, and the attractive spirit of Katie King, her arm linked in his. . . Such photographs as these eventually became an embarrassment to the scientist, for his fellow workers tended to laugh at him for believing in ghosts. Eventually he decided not to insist on trying to persuade such people of the existence of ghosts, though he himself never lost interest in spiritualism.

One might think that when Sir William died it would have been the end of his work for spiritualism. He had left some very useful reports of a highly scientific nature on the importance of spirits, as well as a whole range of books on the subject, but even this was not the end of this remarkable man.

Three years ago a journalist friend asked me if I would like to meet a woman who specialized in automatic writing, of the kind which is described in the story about the monks of Glastonbury. She had told my friend that she was in contact with the spirit of Sir William Crookes. Knowing of my interest in all such matters he suggested we call on her. Naturally I went—and found that her house in London was in the same Holland Park square as the one where Sir William had lived and died. I took several photographs that afternoon, mainly ones of the lady working at her automatic writing, but my main interest was in photographing the words which were being written under the influence of Sir William. I photographed the final sheet of a letter, 'written' while I was there and signed by the spirit of Sir William. When I got home that night, I developed the film and then compared the signature of the spirit writings with a signature on a letter in my possession, which Sir William had written in 1880, nearly forty years before his death. You have guessed what I found? Yes, the two signatures were absolutely identical!

THE WRITING ON THE WALL

Christine Bernard

So far, we have barely touched on dreams that foretell the future. Certainly, a great many have been recorded, and a large number have to do with predictions of disaster and death—though these usually occur too late to be of much use to the unfortunate victims. But other, more cheerful kinds of dreams of prediction have also been recorded, such as the famous case of the fifteenth-century Swaffham Tinker, whose dream led him to crocks of gold buried beneath the only tree in his own back garden! His story is commemorated by a tablet in the market-place of his home-town in Norfolk. It reads: *The tinker of Swaffham who did by a dream find a treasure.*

My own favourite among the many hundreds of dream stories that I have come across is the well-authenticated one about Dr. Herman Hilprecht, a famous oriental scholar who had great knowledge of the ancient kingdoms of Assyria. Born in Germany in 1859, he emigrated to America in 1886 and eventually rose to an important position at the University of Pennsylvania. At one time this learned gentleman was trying to finish, and deliver to his publishers on time, the manuscript of his now famous book, *Old Babylonian Inscriptions.*

To finish it, he had to translate the letters on two small pieces of agate. He knew that they had originally come from the Temple of Baal at Nippur and he believed the pieces had once been rings. But they were so broken, and so small, that the tiny engraved letters were quite unreadable. Tired though he was, Dr. Hilprecht worked late into the night, twisting and turning the agate fragments this way and that, under the most powerful magnifying glass he could find, trying to wrest their secret from them.

At last, still sitting at his desk, he fell asleep. He awoke, or thought he had done so, startled to find a tall man standing beside him. With a shock, he realized that the man was dressed in the long robes of the priests of Baal and looked much like the figures he had seen many times, carved on the ruined temple walls of Assyria. The man said, "Come with me, I will help you". Now the doctor discovered that he was sitting, not at his desk, but on a massive stone step and a hot wind blew about him. He rose and followed the priest along an empty street of deserted buildings. The priest turned into the largest and most splendid of these, which was set a little apart.

"You are in the Temple of Baal at Nippur," said the priest, "which lies between the Rivers

Tigris and Euphrates." Looking round him in the huge, dimly-lit hall, Dr. Hilprecht realised that the archeologists of his own day had been very clever in reconstructing a model of a building very similar to this one, though they had only had a few broken pillars and stones, scattered in the desert, to work from. He turned to the priest.

"Can you tell me where the secret treasure-room of your temple is?" he asked. "No-one since your day has ever been able to discover it."

The priest led him across the main hall and down a long, dark passage, at the end of which was a small, well-protected room. This was empty except for a small wooden chest. When the priest opened it the doctor saw that this too was empty—except for a few fragments of agate.

The priest said that they were part of what had once been a holy cylinder, and that the doctor's own pieces of stone had also come from this cylinder.

"We were once ordered," explained the priest, "to make a pair of agate ear-rings for the god Ninib. But the only agate we could find was this cylinder. So, here in this room it was cut into three pieces. One piece, left over from the ear-rings, was lost." Since each segment carried a part of the original inscription, it was no wonder that Dr. Halprecht had been quite unable to decipher his own fragment.

"And what was this inscription?" cried the doctor in great excitement. "What does it say? Can you tell me?"

"These are holy words," answered the priest, "and they cannot be spoken." He turned to a wall of the little room and in the thick dust that covered it he wrote: Kurigalzu, pontifex* of Baal, has presented this to the god Ninib, son of Baal.

As Dr. Hilprecht read the words, they started to fade; he had hardly finished memorizing them before they had vanished completely. The temple too, vanished, and he found himself back in his study at Philadelphia. Yet the priest still stood beside him. Now, on the desk before them lay a sheet of paper on which was written the word 'Nebuchadnezzar'. Only recently the doctor had been arguing its meaning with two famous Egyptologists who had translated it as 'Nebo, protect my work as a mason'. Somehow, the doctor had not felt this was accurate. The priest glanced at the paper and smiled. "That is wrong," he said gently. "The correct meaning of the name is 'Nebo, protect my boundary'." Then he faded away into the dawn light that streamed through the windows, and Dr. Halprecht awoke.

This story has a most pleasing and satisfactory ending. First, since he now had the missing in-

* A high priest of ancient times.

scription in his possession, Dr. Hilprecht was able to deliver his completed manuscript on time. Later, someone else identified the agate fragments as part of a cylinder, confirming what the priest had told the doctor. Thirdly, his version of the meaning of the name Nebuchadnezzar came to be accepted by modern scholars; and lastly, when another expedition was later sent to the Temple of Baal, the site of the treasure-room was found to be located exactly at the spot where the priest had led the doctor in his dream!

THE BLOODY HAND

Lord Halifax

A widow and her two daughters, Ellen and Mary, were living in a village on the south coast. Their house stood rather apart from its neighbours, situated on a wooded cliff. About a quarter of a mile from the garden was a waterfall of some height. The two daughters were very attached to each other. One of them, Mary, was extremely pretty and attractive. Among her admirers there were two men especially devoted to her, and one of them, John Bodneys, seemed on the point of claiming her hand, when a new suitor appeared and completely conquered Mary's heart.

The day was fixed for the marriage, but though Mary wrote to the Bodneys to announce her engagement and to ask John to be present at her wedding, no reply was received. On the eve of the wedding day, Ellen was gathering ferns in the wood for the house decorations when she heard a faint rustling behind her and, turning quickly round, thought she caught sight of the figure of John Bodneys; but whoever it was vanished swiftly in the twilight. On her return to the house, she told her sister who she thought she had seen, but neither of them thought much of it.

The marriage took place next day. Just before the bride was due to leave with her husband, she took her sister to the room they had shared. The window opened on to a balcony and a flight of steps led down to an enclosed garden. After a few words, Mary said to her sister, "I would like to be alone for a few minutes. I will join you again presently."

Ellen left her and went downstairs, where she waited with the others. When half an hour had passed and Mary had not appeared, her sister went up to see if anything had happened. The bedroom door was locked. Ellen called, but had no answer. She called again more loudly: still no answer. Becoming alarmed, she ran downstairs and told her mother. At last the door was forced open, but there was no trace of Mary in the room. They went into the garden, but except for a white rose lying on the path, nothing was to be seen. For the rest of that day and on the following days everyone hunted high and low. The police were called in, the whole countryside was roused, but all to no purpose. Mary had disappeared completely.

Many years passed by. The mother and Mary's husband were dead, and of the wedding party only Ellen and an old servant were left.

One winter's night the wind rose to a furious gale and did a great deal of damage to the trees near the waterfall. When the workmen came in the morning to clear away the fallen timber and fragments of rock, they came upon a skeleton hand, on the third finger of which was a wedding ring, guarded by another ring with a red stone. On searching further, they found a complete skeleton, round whose dried-up bones some rags of clothes still adhered. The ring with the red stone was identified by Ellen as one which her sister was wearing on her wedding day. The skeleton was given a proper burial in the churchyard, but the shock of the discovery was so great that a few weeks later Ellen, now an old lady, was herself on her death-bed. On the occasion of Mary's burial, she had insisted on keeping the skeleton hand with the rings, putting it in a glass box to secure it from accident; and now when she lay dying, she left the relic to the care of an old man-servant.

Shortly afterwards this servant set up a public-house, where, as may be imagined, the skeleton hand and its story were a common topic of conversation among those who frequented the bar. One night a stranger, muffled up in a cloak and with his cap pulled over his face, arrived at the inn and asked for something to drink.

"It was a night like this when the great oak was blown down," the publican observed to one of his customers.

"Yes," the other replied. "And it must have made the skeleton seem doubly ghastly, discovered as it was in the midst of ruins."

"What skeleton?" asked the stranger, turning suddenly from the corner in which he had been standing.

"Oh, it's a long story," answered the publican. "You can see the hand in that glass case, and if you like, I will tell you how it came there."

He waited for an answer, but none came. The stranger was leaning against the wall in a state of collapse. He was staring at the hand, repeating again and again, "Blood, blood!" Horrified, the publican followed the stricken man's gaze ... to see blood slowly dripping from the fingertips of the hand in the glass case. A few minutes later the man had recovered sufficiently to admit that he was John Bodneys. Immediately he asked to be taken to the magistrates. In spite of the late hour they were called out. When they were gathered he confessed that, in a frenzy of jealousy, he had climbed into the private garden on Mary's wedding day. Seeing her alone in her room, he had entered and seized her, muffling her cries, and had taken her as far as the waterfall. There she had struggled so violently to escape from him that, unintentionally, he had pushed her off the rocks and she had fallen into a cleft where she was almost completely hidden. Afraid of being discovered, he had not even waited to find out whether she were dead or alive. He had fled and had lived abroad ever since, until an overpowering longing led him to revisit the scene of his crime.

After making his confession, Bodneys was committed to the county gaol, where shortly afterwards he died, before any trial could take place.

THE CASE OF THE BELL WITCH

America's most famous ghost story

During the years between 1817 and 1821, there occurred an extraordinary series of ghostly visitations to the John Bell farm in Robertson County, in the State of Tennessee. The 'Witch', as the haunter was called, is a good description because, unlike modern poltergeists who, though given to mischief and destruction, stop short of murder, the Bell Witch did not. It only ceased its activities after the death of John Bell, the head of the household, whom it tortured and persecuted with unrelenting savagery.

The first account of the strange happenings was written in 1846 by Richard Bell, one of John Bell's nine sons. His story was rather like a diary and was called *Our Family Trouble*. His manuscript, however, was not published until very much later, in 1894, when it finally appeared as a book, *An Authentic History of the Famous Bell Witch*.

The disturbances began—as they very often do —with knockings and scrapings at the doors and windows of Bell Farm. If the light was put on, the noise ceased. Then the sound moved inside.

Week after week an invisible 'rat' was gnawing on the bed-post, and an equally invisible 'dog' was clawing on the floor. Something flapped against the ceiling. Sounds were heard as if the beds were suddenly roughly pulled apart; as if dogs chained together were fighting. The noise grew, moving from room to room, only stopping when everybody got up and searched for the cause. About a year after it began, it had so increased that it fairly shook the house. Then the coverings started slipping off the beds; a smacking of lips, a gulping sound, a choking and a strangling noise were heard. Occasionally it seemed as if heavy stones had fallen from somewhere; as if chairs had been overthrown or heavy chains had been dragged across the floor. Some new performance was added every night, and it seemed to trouble Elizabeth, John Bell's daughter, known as Betsy—more than anyone else.

At this stage, the family decided that the secrecy they had observed so far was unwise. They needed help. So they called in Mr. John Johnson, their nearest neighbour and intimate friend, to help solve the mystery. It was Mr. Johnson who made the discovery that behind the phenomena was some intelligence. He listened attentively to all the sounds, and particularly to 'that which appeared like someone sucking air through the teeth', and called to it in the name of the Lord. This silenced the noise for a considerable time, then the persecution of Betsy was renewed with vigour. Her cheeks were frequently crimsoned as if by a hard blow from an open hand, and her hair pulled until she would scream with pain.

Mr. Johnson gathered that 'it' understood the human language, and advised John Bell to invite other friends and form a committee of investigation. From Richard's account it appears that the main job of the committee was to keep a close watch on the family, 'but the demonstrations increased in force, and Sister was so severely punished that Father and Mother became alarmed for her safety when alone, and the neighbouring girls came almost every night to keep her company.' Hoping that it might rid her of the trouble, Betsy was sent to the neighbours; 'but it made no difference; the trouble followed her with the same severity, disturbing the family where she went as it did at home.'

By this time the mystery had become notorious; the house was crowded every night with visitors who tried to make the Witch talk. They called on it 'to rap on the wall, smack its mouth, etc., and in this way it apparently developed.' During this time it was not uncommon to see lights 'like a candle or lamp flitting across the yard and through the field; often when Father, the boys and "hands" were coming in from work, chunks of wood and stones would fall along the way, as if tossed by someone, but we could never discover from whence, or what direction they came.'

Those who tried to stop the covers being pulled off their beds were slapped on the face and beaten up. 'The blows were heard distinctly, like the open palm of a heavy hand, while the sting was keenly felt.' The visitors persisted in urging the Witch to talk, and finally it commenced whistling when spoken to, in a low, broken sound, as if trying to speak. In this way it progressed until the whistling sound was changed to a weak, faltering whisper, uttering indistinct words. The voice gradually gained strength, and soon words became distinct.

This was a sensational development. The voice was not confined to darkness, as were the physical phenomena. The talking was heard in lighted rooms, and finally during the day at any hour. Some people accused Betsy of ventriloquism. John Jr. suggested a test to a visiting doctor. The doctor placed his hand over Betsy's mouth at the time when the voice was heard, and soon satisfied himself that she was in no way connected with these sounds. The reason why this accusation was levelled against Betsy is most interesting. To quote from Richard's account:

'Sister was now subjected to fainting spells followed by shortness of breath and smothering sensations, losing her breath for nearly a minute between gasps, finally becoming unconscious.

97

These spells lasted from thirty to forty minutes, and passed off suddenly, leaving her restored after a few minutes. There is no positive evidence that these spells were produced by the Witch. Though a very stout girl she had robust health, and was never subject to hysteria or such. Moreover, the spells came on at regular hours in the evening, just at the time the Witch usually appeared, and immediately after the spells passed off the mysterious voice commenced talking, but never uttered a word during Betsy's prostration.

In the meantime, Father was strangely afflicted. He complained of a curious sensation in his mouth, a stiffness of the tongue, and something like a stick crosswise, punching each side of his jaws. This sensation did not last long nor often, nor cause pain, and therefore gave him little concern. But as the phenomenon developed, this affliction increased, his tongue swelling against his jaws, so that he could neither talk nor eat for as much as ten or fifteen hours.

In the meanwhile the Witch manifested a vicious dislike for Father, using the most vile and malignant epithets toward him, declaring that it would torment 'Old Jack Bell' to the end of his life. As Father's trouble increased, Elizabeth was gradually relieved from her spells, and soon recovered entirely. But Father was seized with another malady that caused him much trouble and suffering. This was contortions of the face, a twitching and dancing of his flesh, which laid him up for a time.'

"I am a spirit, who was once very happy, but has been disturbed, and made unhappy" were the first words of the Witch, spoken in a feeble but distinct voice. Then it went on to say that it would continue worrying John Bell, and that it would kill him in the end. After much coaxing it gave the neighbour John Johnson (whom it called 'Old Sugar Mouth') a grandiose statement: "I am a Spirit from everywhere, Heaven, Hell, the Earth; I am in the air, in houses, any place at any time, have been created millions of years; that is all I will tell you."

The same childish boasting was noticeable in the statements of the Talking Mongoose (see p. 60) "I am the Fifth Dimension", etc. The Witch first declared itself to be the spirit of an Indian whose bones had been scattered, then it professed to be Old Kate Batts's witch, sending a shudder of delicious horror through its audience. Mrs. Batts was an eccentric old woman, slightly unbalanced and commonly feared as a witch.

The Witch started on its speaking career as a pious character, singing beautiful songs, quoting from the Bible with remarkable knowledge, and reproducing the Sunday sermons of the two local preachers word for word, and with a perfect imitation of the pastor's voice. The memory and mimicry of the Witch were unique. It could assume anybody's voice and it never forgot a thing.

The Witch gave plenty of evidence of a sense of humour. It sent the members of the Bell family on a fake treasure-hunt, and enjoyed the leg-pull immensely. But it was also willing to be of service to the family and gave them good advice. Like the Talking Mongoose (see p. 59), it was a magnificent reporter, collecting gossip from all over the countryside and becoming the holy terror of evil-doers. It denounced the drunkards, abused those who whipped their children, read the thoughts of those present, revealed unpleasant secrets of their past, and followed and spied on them.

Before the disturbances began, John Bell saw a peculiar animal sitting between two rows of corn. It looked like a dog, yet it was not. He shot at the animal which at once disappeared. It was later assumed that this animal was the Witch. Later Drewry and Betsy saw another strange animal creature; then oddly behaving rabbits were seen, and the Witch, now being able to talk, duly claimed their shape as its own. It is interesting to note that no one actually saw the Witch in human shape; and it seemed to have no knowledge of its own sex, never referring to itself as being either male or female.

Poltergeists can produce odd objects in a mysterious way, apparently from thin air. The

Witch was no exception. It joined Mrs. Bell's Bible readings and 'when refreshments were served it always brought in nice fruits that were simply dropped on the table or in their laps with the invitation to eat them. At Betsy's birthday party the Witch called out: "I have a surprise for you; come and see it." Suddenly a large basket of fruit—oranges, bananas, grapes and nuts— was placed on the table by unseen hands. The Spirit called: "Those came from the West Indies. I brought them myself." '

When Mrs. Bell fell ill, the Witch was disconsolate: Richard described how, 'it's plaintive voice was heard exclaiming: "Luce, poor Luce, how do you feel now? Hold out your hands, Luce, and I will give you something." Mother stretched out her arms and hazelnuts were dropped from above into her hands. This was witnessed by several ladies who had called to see Mother, and it was so incredible that the floor above was examined. After some time the amazement was increased by the same voice inquiring: "Say, Luce, why don't you eat the hazelnuts?" Mother replied that she could not crack them. Then the voice exclaimed: "Well, I will crack some for you," and instantly the sound of cracking was heard, and cracked nuts dropped on her bed within hand's reach. Next came the grapes in the same way, the voice begging her to eat them, that they would do her good.'

One day a famous leader in the War of Independence, General Andrew Jackson, announced that he was coming to visit the Bells. As the carriage drove up to the house, the horses suddenly became unable to pull it along, although the wheels were on level ground. The General shouted: "By the Eternal, boys, it is the Witch." Then came a sharp metallic voice from the bushes saying: "All right, General, let it move." And the carriage moved on.

Time passed and the children grew up, and Betsy became engaged to a local boy. But the Witch changed little. It always showed the tenderest regard for Elizabeth's mother. She was 'the most perfect woman living'—yet the hostility towards Betsy and her father continued. The Witch actually broke up Betsy's engagement to Joshua Gardner. They were ideally suited, but the Witch objected to the match from the moment it learned to talk. In a soft, melancholy voice, sighing in the distance and gradually approaching nearer, with gentle, whispering pleadings, it said, "please Betsy Bell, don't have Joshua Gardner, please Betsy Bell, don't marry Joshua Gardner!" The voice was so sweet, yet so very mystifying that it not only bewildered the young lovers but brought confusion into the family circle. As time passed, the Witch grew sharper and sharper. It said so many things to Betsy and Joshua of a highly embarrassing

102

nature that the girl became quite hysterical and worn out with despair.

Now we come to the saddest, and indeed the nastiest part of the story. After a period of comparative peace, the Witch renewed its attacks upon the father of the Bell family. Four years after the hauntings began, she brought to a climax her plans—if plans they were. His attacks occurred more frequently, his face jerking and twitching, his tongue becoming so swollen that his whole face was distorted. Each spell would last from one to two days, and the Witch grew ever angrier. Every word uttered to John was a blast of curses and threats, while those uttered to Betsy's mother continued to be loving and kind. During a severe attack, which confined John Bell to bed for six or seven days, 'the Witch cursed and raved like a maniac for several days and ceased not troubling him'. After he got better, the Witch attacked him in the open air. His shoes were repeatedly jerked off, a phenomenon which his son Richard saw with his own eyes and later recorded.

'Presently Father complained of a blow on his face which felt like an open hand that almost stunned him, and he sat down on a log that lay by the roadside. Then his face commenced jerking with fearful contortions. Soon his whole body; and then his shoes would fly off as fast as I could put them on . . . Having finished tying

Father's shoes, I heard the sound of derisive songs piercing the air. As the demoniac shrieks died away, the spell passed off and I saw tears chasing down Father's quivering cheeks.'

On returning to the house, John Bell took to his bed and from then on gradually declined. On the 19th December, 1820, he was discovered in a deep stupor and could not be aroused. John Jr. went to the medicine cupboard and, instead of the bottle for which he was looking, found 'a smokey-looking vial, which was about one-third full of dark-coloured liquid'. The doctor was immediately sent for, and in the meantime the Witch was heard in joyous exultation: "It's useless for you to try to relieve Old Jack—I have got him this time; he will never get up from that bed again." Asked about the medicine found in the cupboard, the Witch replied: "I put it there and gave Old Jack a big dose out of it last night while he was fast asleep, which fixed him."

When the doctor arrived, it was suggested that a test be made of the contents of the vial. A straw was run into it and wiped on the tongue of a cat. 'The cat jumped and whirled over a few times, stretched out, kicked and died very quick.' The vial and contents were thrown into the fire, and instantly a blue haze shot up the chimney like a flash of powder.

John Bell died the following morning. The Witch 'was there, indulging in wild exultations and derisive songs.' At the burial, after the grave was filled and the friends turned to leave, the Witch broke out in a loud voice, singing a popular drinking ballad of the day: 'Row me up some brandy O', and continued singing this until the family and friends had all returned to the house.

With the killing of poor John Bell, the days of the Witch were numbered. Richard says that 'there were but two purposes, seemingly, developed in the visitation. One was the persecution of Father to the end of his life. The other, the vile purpose of destroying the anticipated happiness of Betsy.' During the rest of the winter and the spring the visits lessened, as if the energy that fed the Witch had gradually run out. The final phenomenon took place as the family was sitting round the fire after their evening meal. 'Something like a cannon-ball rolled down the chimney and out into the room, bursting like a smoke ball. A voice clearly called out: "I am going, and will be gone for seven years. Goodbye to all." '

And indeed the return took place as predicted. Mrs. Bell and her sons Joel and Richard were the only occupants of the house. Betsy was now married—though not to Joshua. But this time the manifestations consisted only of scratching sounds and the pulling-off of the covers of the beds. The family agreed to ignore the disturbances, and the Witch departed in two weeks without causing further trouble. It paid two visits to John Jr. at his home, and promised to return again 'in one hundred years and seven' to one of John's descendants. This doubtful honour should have fallen on a Dr. Charles Bailey Bell, but the year of 1935 came and went, and the Bell Witch failed to keep its tryst.

PRESIDENT LINCOLN'S DREAM

Lord Halifax

The story of Abraham Lincoln's dream on the night before his murder is very famous. The politician, Gideon Welles, one of the members of Lincoln's cabinet, has left this account of the President's description of the dream:

'He said it had to do with water, that he seemed to be in a strange vessel, and that he was moving rapidly towards a dark shore. He had had the dream several times and was always in the same mysterious vessel, he said. He dreamed it before the battles of Bull Run, Gettysburg, Stone River, Wilmington, etc., Victory did not always follow his dream, but the events and their results were always of the utmost importance.'

The next day, Friday, April 13th, 1865, he was assassinated by an actor, John Wilkes Booth.

A famous English novelist heard a slightly different account from an eye witness. Charles Dickens went on a tour of America in 1867 and, among many other places, he visited Washington, where he called upon his friend Charles Sumner, a Senator. He particularly wanted to meet a friend of Sumner's, an American general called Edwin Stanton, so the Senator arranged for the three men to dine together at his house.

Towards midnight, before they separated, Stanton turned to Sumner and said: "Before I go, I should very much like to tell Charles about the President's dream, because I know he's always interested in things relating to the occult."

"Of course," said Sumner, pleased on his guest's behalf. "Why not do so now? The hour is most suitable!"

So Stanton gave his account of the President's last night alive. "During the Civil War," he said, "I was in charge of all the troops in Columbia, and, as you may imagine, I had my hands pretty full. One day there was a council called for two o'clock, but I was busy and could not get there until twenty minutes later. When I entered my colleagues were looking rather grave, but I thought nothing of it—those were grave times—nor did I take much notice as I entered of what the President was saying which was to the effect that it had nothing to do with the business in hand, and that now I had arrived they must get on. Various matters were discussed and settled. At the end of the meeting I walked out with the Attorney General, saying, "Well, we have really done some work today. The President got down to business and really applied himself to it, instead of flitting from chair to chair, talking to all and sundry, as he sometimes does."

"Ah," said the Attorney General, "but you do

not know what he said before you arrived?"

"No, please tell me."

"When we entered the Council Chamber to-day," he replied, "we found the President seated at the top of the table with his face buried in his hands. We did not dare speak, but presently he raised his head and we saw that he looked grave and worn. He said, 'Gentlemen, before long you will have serious news.' We all asked what had happened, what bad news had he received. 'I have no news for I have heard nothing—but you will hear tomorrow.'"

"Again we pressed him to tell us what had happened and at last he said, 'I have had a dream. I have dreamed that dream three times: once before the battle of Bull Run, once on another occasion—and again last night. I am in a boat, a strange boat, on a boundless ocean. I have no oars, no rudder'—and here the President groaned terribly—'I am helpless. I drift, I drift, I drift!'"

"Five hours later," said Edwin Stanton gravely, "the President was assassinated."

THE GHOSTS OF BILLINGHAM MANOR

Billingham Manor lies on the Isle of Wight near the village of Godshill, surrounded by beautiful vistas and walled gardens. Charles I had friends there, the Worsley family, whom he frequently visited. In 1647 they were busy planning his escape to France. The King was being held prisoner at nearby Carisbrooke Castle, though he was allowed a great deal of freedom, and the Worsleys planned that the king should hide in one of the secret cupboards in the Manor, which connected with several underground passages, some running hundreds of yards out to the open country. Horses would be waiting for him and he would be taken to Chale Bay. There a boat would carry him to France and his exiled family. Alas, Charles decided that it would be unseemly for a king to behave like a fugitive and he refused to take part in the plan. In September 1648 an armed force took him across the Solent to Hurst Castle—and four months later the 'White King' lost his head in Whitehall.

In 1722 the Manor was rebuilt in the fashion of the time; a young Worsley then inherited it, and married the beautiful daughter of a neighbour, a Miss Leigh, although the union was against her wishes. She was in love with a young French nobleman whom she continued to meet in secret after her marriage. One day Worsley discovered them together and instantly challenged the Frenchman to a duel. They fought in the walled garden, it is said, and the Frenchman was killed. Afterwards, Worsley forbade his wife to leave the house. Confined to the morning room, she was only allowed to visit the kitchen once a day to give orders to the cook. It is said that Mrs. Worsley, clad in a grey cloak, haunts the Manor. The scent of Madonna lilies accompanies her appearances. The mortally wounded Frenchman had been carried into the house to die, and since then his ghost, too, is said to haunt the house, while the rattling of a sword and the clash of metal have been several times heard, as we shall relate.

Sir Shane Leslie, the writer, and his wife and family took the Manor as a holiday home in the summer of 1929, and their servants went with them. They all travelled to the Isle of Wight by sea and by road from their native Ireland. They were delighted with the gardens when they arrived, and the children were particularly thrilled by the panelling of the old rooms which led to secret stairs. The day they moved in, Lady Leslie was shown over the house by the owner. She had never believed in ghosts, yet, as they walked down the long passage from the library, a strange feeling came over her. To her surprise, she heard herself ask: "There aren't any ghosts here, are there?" The owner replied rather guardedly, that she was sure the family wouldn't be disturbed by "anything of *that* kind!" and with this she had to be content.

The largest bedroom—a corner room of faded chintzes, smelling of lavender—Lady Leslie chose for herself. The first night, when preparing to sleep in its old-fashioned four-poster, she found herself glancing repeatedly over her shoulder, feeling the presence of someone else in the room. Once in bed, she tried to read, feeling all the time that there was a corner of the room she must watch. "A kind of fear that I hadn't felt since I was six years old came over me," she later related. "I pulled the bedclothes up under my chin, beads of perspiration covered my upper lip. I didn't turn the light off, and there I lay until dawn—explaining to myself that I must have some kind of nervous insomnia caused by travel fatigue."

The parlour-maid's appearance with the breakfast tray the following morning was a relief. However, when asked by her mistress how she had slept, she was quick to answer for all the servants. Not one of them, she said, had had a good night. In fact, each had dragged her mattress into the parlour-maid's room, and slept on the floor.

Later that day Lady Leslie went to meet her sister Anne, who had just arrived from New

York. Anne was given a room in the more modern part of the manor. Yvonne, Anne's French maid, who spoke no English and had never been in England before, was given a room adjoining her mistress's.

Asked the following morning how she had slept, Anne was almost too ashamed to say. "I cannot imagine what happened to me, but I never closed my eyes till dawn. I was frightened, for no known reason, and didn't even dare to put out my light . . . and Yvonne, who doesn't like the country anyway, says that something was moving around her room all night, and she wants to change it."

No sooner had Lady Leslie moved her sister into a smaller room than her own maid, who, up till now, had been strangely silent, said to her, "Madam, there was something moving about in my room last night. It not only rustled the tissue-paper from the trunks, but there were things like hands that groped over me, and pressed on my chest."

"Nonsense!" replied Lady Leslie. "It must have been the house cat that was left behind, and misses its owner!"

The rest of the day, spent partly by the sea and partly in the garden, passed pleasantly; and everybody retired to bed thoroughly tired and contented. Jack Leslie, who was nine, occupied a room next to his mother's. A heavy washstand which stood across the communicating door prevented access to Jack's room. In order to turn on the light in the hall upstairs, it was necessary to grope one's way to the switch by the head of the stairs.

Suddenly, in the small hours of the next night, there came from Jack's room the most terrific commotion. It sounded as though bodies were being hurled about, and thumpings struck the wall just by the head of Lady Leslie's bed. "Jacky!" she shouted, "what's the matter?" She was answered by two dull thuds in the hall. Jumping out of bed and rushing to the connecting door to listen for any response from her son, she felt, close to her ear, a brushing and groping on the door, as of the shoulder and hands of somebody trying to find the handle. "Who's there?" she cried, shooting the bolt, and vigorously striking the door with her fist. This was immediately answered by a powerful thump on the other side, and then by a metallic sound such as might have been made by a sword being withdrawn from its scabbard. "My hair stood on end. I rushed for my crucifix, and, with this in one hand and a poker in the other, prepared for any emergency. I sat on my bed, smoking one cigarette after another, while thumps, now loud, now low, like furniture being moved, went on, up and down the dark hall, for some minutes. Ghosts never entered my head, but that some evil doer had broken into the house, I was certain." Yet to her amazement, when she eventually found the courage to examine the house, she found her children sleeping peacefully, quite undisturbed. "Nothing was touched, no chairs nor tables were overturned, the silver remained in the dining-room, the doors and windows were all locked. I went outside and examined the flower-beds under the windows, and found no foot-prints."

Next day, when cook came for her orders, she locked the door behind her, rolled her eyes, and told her mistress that she wanted to speak with her privately. *Someone was in the house last night,* she said.

"But Mrs. Carr, we're miles from anywhere, in the safest and best policed place on earth, and no one could escape from the island as there is only the one boat."

Mrs. Carr insisted that not only had *she* heard somebody, but so also had Milly, one of the maids. Indeed, Mrs. Carr declared that, while this somebody walked up and down the hall, she actually *spoke* to him! She mentioned that she had no reason to be afraid "as he was a gentle-man with a most beautiful voice." "It's all-l-l-l r-r-right!" he answered softly, when she asked who was there.

A day or two later, Nannie, who occupied a room halfway up the hall with Dermot, the Leslies' younger son, asked Lady Leslie whether she had been ill in the night. Nannie thought it strange when assured that she had not been. She was not a nervous person, but the night before, she had felt uneasy—so much so that, as her bedroom lock had no key in it, she had pushed a couple of heavy chairs against the door. In the middle of the night she was disturbed by footsteps as of someone pacing up and down the hall. At first she thought it must be Lady Leslie or her sister, trying to find the bathroom. She called out but received no reply. Slowly the latch of her door was lifted. Slowly the door opened, pushing back both chairs. Suddenly, there was a thud as if somebody had fallen in the hall. Nannie now looked out into the dark passage, fully expecting to find there, upon the floor, a fainted figure in a nightgown. There was nothing but empty darkness, black emptiness. *The air, however, was heavy with the scent of flowers— of Madonna lilies.*

One day, Lady Leslie attended a tea-party on the island. She asked her hostess, who had rented a small house some distance away, why she had never thought of renting Billingham Manor. Her question, heard by the other guests, was greeted by an exchange of glances. "Don't be afraid to tell me the truth!" Lady Leslie said, noticing this. As it was now obvious to everybody that she had suspected something, her hostess proceeded to explain. The house, she said, was haunted by a ghost that left the odour of Madonna lilies.

Their only near neighbours lived in a farmhouse and had been there for generations. They would not speak of ghosts, nor would any of them sleep at the Manor as caretakers. But one day they showed the Leslies a photograph of the Manor dining-room. Written on the back was the caption: 'The uninvited guest. A snapshot taken before Miss Martha's wedding breakfast, March, 1902.' The picture shows a large table, with a huge wedding cake filling the centre, surrounded by flowers. The room is empty, except for a shadowy figure; standing by the table, and looking down at it is a man in a white wig, with ruffles at his neck and wrists. The panelled wall could clearly be seen through his shadowy body. On his face is an expression of great sadness. Could he have been the slain lover, now 'the skeleton at the feast'? Perhaps his spirit was aroused by the wedding celebrations, reminding him of the marriage he never had . . .

The Leslies managed to stay out their agreed term at Billingham. At sundown on the evening before their departure Lady Leslie stood on the path just outside the old front door watching Jacky shoot an arrow from the lawn. The boy turned his head toward her. His jaw dropped; and his face wore a stunned expression. "Mummy," he said, "did you see that?"

"See what?" she asked.

"That thing that was floating right by you. I thought it was smoke; but it had a man's face on the top of it."

Then, unconcernedly, he shot his arrow into the air.

J. B. Priestley, the famous writer, acquired Billingham Manor in the 'thirties. In 1946 a friend, the author Jan de Hartog, took his publisher there for a brief visit. Having shown him over the house, de Hartog said that he would now lock up the house and return the key to the Lodge.

"What about the housekeeper?" enquired the publisher. "Can't she do that?"

De Hartog said that there was no housekeeper in residence, since the Priestley family were in London.

"Then do you mind telling me who the lady is?"

Bewildered, de Hartog replied, "What lady?"

"What?" cried the publisher, "you mean you didn't see her? Why, she was standing by the front door, and each time we passed she smiled kindly at us!"

The author assured him the house was empty and he'd seen nothing, but the publisher insisted that he had clearly seen a lady in a grey cloak quietly standing near the door—not once but several times. As can be imagined, both men left hastily!

THE JINXED TOURING CAR

Christine Bernard

The powerful and famous Hapsburgh family ruled over large areas of Europe for hundreds of years. They fought, looted and married their way to power until, during the nineteenth and twentieth centuries, Franz Joseph I ruled over a vast territory that included parts of Yugoslavia, Hungary and Austria. However, in his greed for land and money (though, to be fair, he was not much worse in this than other contemporary rulers) he made many enemies. Finally, a curse was laid on him and his family—some say by a Hungarian priest—and an incredible saga of accident, violence, madness and death followed. (To name only two incidents, his son Rudolph committed suicide and his wife was stabbed to death by anarchist).

One day in June, 1914, the Emperor's heir, the Archduke Franz Ferdinand, and his wife, while on a visit to review military manoeuvres in what is now called Yugoslavia, were driving in a parade through the town of Sarajevo. They rode in a very grand, dark green touring car, a Gräf und Stift, owned by the Count Harrach. The whole of Europe at that time was in a state of turmoil; anarchy and rebellion were rife and South-East Europe in particular was in deep political trouble. Suddenly, from the crowd a young revolutionary stepped forward, raised his gun and shot both the Archduke and his wife. The assassination triggered off local uprisings and within two months World War I had broken out in earnest.

However, the murder of the Emperor's heir was only the first in another separate chain of disasters that were to be linked with the dark green touring car—for apparently this vehicle had been cursed as well. After the shooting tragedy, the car was garaged in the house of the Governor of Sarajevo. Soon after the war got under way a General Oscar Potiorek, Commander of the Fifth Austrian Corps, seized the Governor's house—and his car. He commandeered it immediately for his own use. Exactly twenty-one days later he was catastrophically defeated in an engagement and lost his command as a result. Sent back to Vienna in disgrace, the General lived there in illness and poverty. Finally, he lost his reason and died in a workhouse for the poor.

A young captain who had served with the General was the car's next owner. Nine days later he was driving along a country lane. He ran over and killed two farm-workers, swerved into a tree, broke up the car, and was found to be dead when taken out of the wreckage. You feel you can breathe a sigh of relief that the car had been smashed up? Far from it. It was laboriously repaired and again garaged, no doubt being too expensive to run during war-time. The new Governor of Yugoslavia became its next owner. He had four accidents in four months while driving this car, finally losing his arm in one of them. He ordered the destruction of the car, but a Dr. Srkis, who was much intrigued by the idea of owning such a historic vehicle, persuaded the Governor to sell it to him. A modern rationalist, the doctor was convinced that no sane person could possibly believe in such an absurd curse—a jinxed motor-car indeed! Its reputation, he said, was founded merely on a series of tragic coincidences.

For the next six months it seemed that he was right. Then the car was found at the side of the road. Only slightly damaged, it was upside down for no reason that anyone ever discovered. When it was turned the right way up, Dr. Srkis was found crushed to death beneath it.

It was sold to a wealthy jeweller, who drove it without incident for a year. It is interesting that as time passed the curse seemed to be taking longer to wreak its vengeance on the car's owner. However, the jeweller then committed suicide. Another doctor bought it, but because his patients, nervous of the car's curse, started to leave him, he sold it before any harm came to him.

Its next owner was a Swiss racing driver. He decided to use it in a racing competition in the Dolomite Mountains. During the race the car ran off the road, and hit a stone wall. The driver was catapulted over it and killed instantly.

Next, a wealthy Sarajevo farmer bought it, had it repaired—and drove it again for several months, without harm or injury. One morning it broke down, and no efforts could get it to start again. So the farmer asked a passing driver to give him a tow into the city to have it mended. Just as the driver was pulling out of the farm, the engine of the green car roared into life, the car leapt forward, snapping the tow-rope, and hurtled down the road. It overturned on a sharp bend, where the owner was thrown out and killed.

It is unbelievable—yet true, that battered though it was, yet another man was prepared to risk his life for ownership of the green car. Tibor Hirshfeld was a garage proprietor who bought it, repaired it, painted it blue—perhaps this was an attempt to break the jinx?—and drove about in it. One day he was driving six friends to a wedding party when he crashed into another car. Hirshfeld and four of his friends died in the accident.

Then the Austrian Government, probably because of the car's link with the assassinated Archduke Ferdinand, had the car repaired—but this time it was housed in a Vienna Museum, where it was unlikely to do any more damage. It had caused the death of fourteen people, had contributed to the start of the worst war of all time—and was itself supposedly destroyed in another war. A bomb dropped by an Allied plane during World War II fell on the museum —and, it was presumed, the car was smashed to pieces. Presumably, only then was the curse finally exorcised.

This, then, should have been the end of the story. But when writing this account, something nagged away at the back of my mind. A memory came back to me of objects on display at a war museum in Vienna. I was sure I had read something about relics of the start of the First World War. . . Our own Imperial War Museum were extremely helpful and their information led me to a series of photographs, taken *after* the Second World War. The War Museum in Vienna have the state uniform of the Archduke Franz Ferdinand, worn on his last day alive and, as you can see in Plate 4, it was the selfsame car that had carried the Duke and his wife to their death in June, 1914, before starting on its career of death and destruction. Its upholstery gleaming, its brass-work shining, it is *still* on display in the museum, in spite of its war-time shake up. Well, they say the devil looks after his own . . . and I am quite certain that, when I go there, I shall stand well back from its polished exterior!

Armada Ghost Books Nos. 1-14

What is a ghost?

A photographic image on the air? A wandering soul restlessly seeking peace? No one knows for certain. But they certainly send those icy shivers down your spine when you read about them!

There are fourteen Armada Ghost Books, edited by Christine Bernard and Mary Danby—each one a collection of creepy tales to thrill all ghost-lovers (or haters!). Meet moaning spectres, weird phantoms and awful apparitions which will make you shiver with delight— and shudder in terror!

Collect them all, with their colourful and exciting jackets, and enter the strange, eerie world of *gho-o-o-o-sts*!

Armada

From Alfred Hitchcock,

Master of Mystery and Suspense—

A thrilling series of detection and adventure. Meet The
Three Investigators – Jupiter Jones, Peter Crenshaw and Bob
Andrews. Their motto, "We Investigate Anything", leads
the boys into some extraordinary situations – even Jupiter's
formidable brain-power is sometimes stumped by the bizarre
crimes and weird villains they encounter. But with the
occasional piece of advice from The Master himself, The
Three Investigators solve a whole lot of sensational mysteries.

1. The Secret of Terror Castle
2. The Mystery of the Stuttering Parrot
3. The Mystery of the Whispering Mummy
4. The Mystery of the Green Ghost
5. The Mystery of the Vanishing Treasure
6. The Secret of Skeleton Island
7. The Mystery of the Fiery Eye
8. The Mystery of the Silver Spider
9. The Mystery of the Screaming Clock
10. The Mystery of the Moaning Cave
11. The Mystery of the Talking Skull
12. The Mystery of the Laughing Shadow
13. The Secret of the Crooked Cat
14. The Mystery of the Coughing Dragon
15. The Mystery of the Flaming Footprints
16. The Mystery of the Nervous Lion
17. The Mystery of the Singing Serpent
18. The Mystery of the Shrinking House
19. The Secret of Phantom Lake
20. The Mystery of Monster Mountain
21. The Secret of the Haunted Mirror
22. The Mystery of the Dead Man's Riddle
23. The Mystery of the Invisible Dog
24. The Mystery of Death Trap Mine
25. The Mystery of the Dancing Devil
26. The Mystery of the Headless Horse
27. The Mystery of the Magic Circle
28. The Mystery of the Deadly Double

Armada

LINDA CRAIG
MYSTERIES

by ANN SHELDON

Now there's a thrilling new mystery series in Armada.

Linda Craig loves horses – and adventure! Together, she and her beautiful palomino pony, Chica d'Oro, find themselves caught up in all kinds of dangerous escapades – chasing cut-throat horse thieves through underground caverns, roaring down mountain passes after death-dealing smugglers, treasure-hunting in the burning desert – and much more. Make sure you don't miss Linda's first action-packed adventures.

1. The Palomino Mystery
2. The Clue on the Desert Trail
3. The Secret of Rancho del Sol
4. The Mystery of Horseshoe Canyon

If you like Nancy Drew, you'll love Linda Craig!

Armada

Armada Monster Books Nos. 1-6

Edited by R. Chetwynd-Hayes

Meet dozens of the most fearsome creatures ever to have
menaced the earth – or slithered out of the sea – in six
bumper collections of monster stories.

Monsters like Dimblebee's Dinosaur, frozen for centuries
. . . The Sad Vampire, who didn't like blood . . . The
terrible, three-headed Chimaera . . . The awful underwater
menace at Hell's Mouth . . . The appalling Thing in the
Pond . . . The loathsome Lambton Worm . . . The smiling
Green Thing with the human head . . . The dreaded,
death-dealing Water Horse . . . The Gargoyle that came
knocking at the door . . . and lots more mysterious,
marvellous, murderous monsters.

How many Armada Spinechillers have you got?

Armada

CAPTAIN ARMADA

has a whole shipload of exciting books for you

Here are just some of the best-selling titles that Armada has to offer:

- ☐ **6th Armada Ghost Book** Mary Danby 85p
- ☐ **14th Armada Ghost Book** Mary Danby 85p
- ☐ **Animal Ghosts** Carolyn Lloyd 75p
- ☐ **1st Armada Monster Book** R. Chetwynd-Hayes 85p
- ☐ **6th Armada Monster Book** R. Chetwynd-Hayes 85p
- ☐ **The Restless Bones and Other True Mysteries** Peter Haining 85p
- ☐ **The Vampire Terror and Other True Mysteries** Peter Haining 85p
- ☐ **The Mystery of the Magic Circle** Alfred Hitchcock 85p
- ☐ **The Mystery of the Deadly Double** Alfred Hitchcock 85p
- ☐ **The Phantom of Pine Hill** Carolyn Keene 85p